THE
SPORTS
DIVING
MEDICAL

J. L. Publications
PO Box 381, Carnegie, Victoria 3163, Australia
Telephone/Facsimile: 61-3-569 4803

National Library of Australia Cataloguing-in-Publication Data

Parker, John, 1949-
   The Sports Diving Medical
   Bibliography
   Includes Index
   ISBN 0 9590306 8 9.

1. Submarine Medicine. 2. Diving, Submarine-Physiological Aspects.
3. Scuba Diving – Accidents and Injuries. 4. Scuba Diving – Safety Measures.
I. Title.

616.98022

Desktop Publishing
and Cover Design by: Allegro Graphics Pty Ltd, Melbourne. Telephone: 836 1600.
Printed in Australia by: McPherson's Printing Group.

THE SPORTS DIVING MEDICAL

A GUIDE TO MEDICAL CONDITIONS RELEVANT TO SCUBA DIVING

by
Dr. John Parker

J. L. Publications
(A division of Submariner Publications Pty. Ltd.)

J. L. Publications Melbourne

This book is dedicated to
Jefferson C. Davis (1932-1989)
who started the ball rolling.

The Division of Workplace Health and Safety, Queensland
has assisted in the publication of this book to improve
health and safety in Queensland diving workplaces
by providing a much needed resource for medical
practitioners assessing diving candidates fitness.

Foreword

CE: I cannot believe that Parker was silly enough to write a book on diving medical examinations.

DG: It is badly needed.

CE: Agreed, but there is no way that I would have tackled such a task.

DG: You could not have done it.

CE: I know. I certainly would not mean to get dragged into the inevitable controversies.

DG: Oh well, he is young.

The above conversation could not, of course, have taken place. Diving physicians treat each other with far more respect. Nevertheless, had such a discussion transpired, it would have highlighted the major characteristic of this text. It is a text of controversy.

There is no way that it could be otherwise, without becoming bland and uninformative. Dr. John Parker has tackled many complex diving medical problems with expertise and enthusiasm.

Because there are so many controversies in this field, and often so little factual data on which to make a balanced judgement, personal preferences abound. So many individuals, often because of their own personal health experience, will wish to promote or refute different aspects of the diving medical.

It is necessary to weigh the pros and cons of each aspect of the diving medical exam and the influence of each illness on both the diver and his environment. Dr. Parker has managed to achieve this, to maintain an objectivity throughout the text, and to present opposing attitudes when they are indicated.

There is no diving physician who will agree with every statement in the text, nor could there be. Nevertheless, this is one of the most balanced approaches to the diving medical examination that we have encountered. It is a worthy successor to the brilliant text of Dr. Jefferson Davis, and we are pleased to see that John has dedicated the book to that pioneer in this field.

The book will be of value to both diving physicians and diving instructors. The latter may not appreciate the amount of work and consideration that has been put into the text, but the diving physician certainly will.

We are privileged to have been associated with the reviewing of the text and we heartily endorse it for use by all recreational diving medical examiners.

Carl Edmonds
MB, BS, MRCP (Lond), FRACP, MRC Psych,
FRANZCP, FACOM, Dip DHM.
Director, Diving Medical Centre, Sydney.
Consultant in Diving Medicine
to Royal Australian Navy.

Des Gorman
BSc, MD, FAFOM, PhD, Dip DHM.
Director of Medical Services
Royal New Zealand Navy.
Consultant to Royal Australian Navy
and Royal Adelaide Hospital.
President, South Pacific Underwater Medicine
Society (SPUMS).

This book has been compiled using extensive literature search, personal experience and wide discussions with fellow diving doctors and divers.

If you think, know, or think you know of a medical condition relevant to diving which is not included, or can add to a condition included, please write down your comments and send them to the author.

If you have an interesting case history which illustrates a point or a dilemma again, please write to the author.

Full acknowledgments will be included in future editions.

The address for correspondence is:
Dr John Parker
PO Box 207, Airlie Beach, Queensland 4802 Australia.

Contents

Preface

The number of people participating in scuba diving is growing every year. No longer is it only for self-motivated enthusiasts. The diving industry is actively selling the sport to increase its market.

This ever widening diving population contains many people with pre-existing medical conditions who would never be permitted in commercial or military diving.

In the past, diving medicals, especially in sports diving, have been subject to much personal prejudice, leading to inconsistent medical interpretations and loss of reliability and credibility in the diving industry.

Information on the many conditions which are relevant in scuba diving is widely scattered throughout the scientific journals. This book is designed to rectify that situation.

There are wide gaps in our knowledge of the physiology and pathology of diving-related problems. By combining what we do know with common sense and experience it should be possible to give a balanced, consistent medical opinion on fitness to dive.

This handbook is not intended to be a textbook, but is a guide to the diving medical and medical conditions relevant to scuba diving. It assumes some knowledge of diving physics, physiology and medicine. Any doctor conducting a diving medical is strongly recommended to complete a basic course in fitness to dive. Doctors who have not attended such a course are strongly recommended to read basic texts on the subject. The author would recommend: (1) **Diving Medicine for Scuba Divers** *by Edmonds, McKenzie and Thomas* – a simple, straightforward basic explanation of the subject; and (2) **Diving and Subaquatic Medicine** *by Edmonds, Lowry and Pennefather* – a more complete and advanced text.

For other useful references see Appendix D.

DISCLAIMER

Recommendations have been made by the author regarding fitness to dive. These are only the author's opinion and should not be taken as gospel. If there is any doubt about a person's fitness to dive, the doctor should refer the case to someone more experienced in diving medicine.

In addition, since diving medicine is a relatively new and fast-developing field, the reader is strongly advised to read new literature as it is released and, if necessary, to reassess areas of this book accordingly.

The Sport

Scuba diving is unique. It is vastly different from all other sports.

points to ponder

- **The underwater environment is physically demanding**
  - it is not breathable. An artificial air supply is required.
  - it moves. Tides, currents and waves can change conditions dramatically.
  - it contains alien life forms. Some are dangerous, some are perceived as dangerous.
- **The underwater environment exposes the body to numerous stresses**
  - **exercise** loads can be heavy and change suddenly. It is easy to get lost underwater and have to swim far greater distances than planned.
  - **cold** stress occurs both quickly – immersing the face in cold water which induces a reflex slowing of the heart; and slowly – most divers get cold, especially towards the end of the dive.
  - **anxiety** occurs, especially in the novice but also in the experienced.
  - **pressure.** All the air spaces in the body must continually adjust to the surrounding water pressure.
  - **sensory deprivation.**

    reduced vision
    The mask restricts peripheral vision.
    Water visibility can deteriorate suddenly during a dive, especially when a group of novice divers are in the same area and kick up the silt with their fins.
    The visual horizon can be lost.
    Colours are lost with depth.
    It gets darker with depth.

    reduced hearing
    Water in the ear or a hood may occlude the ear.
    Reduced localisation of sound.

    reduced touch
    From gloves or cold hands.

    reduced balance
    Weightlessness can disturb balance and confuse the senses.

    smell and taste
    Although not lost, play little part underwater.
  - **upsidedown positions.** When weightless, the body can be easily placed in unusual positions while the body contents are still subject to gravity.

- **Breathing air at high pressure can have harmful effects**
  - **nitrogen narcosis** – nitrogen becomes narcotic with depth.
  - **decompression sickness** – nitrogen bubbles can form in the tissues.
  - **carbon dioxide toxicity** – breathing against a resistance can cause a build up of carbon dioxide, especially with exertion and at depth due to the mechanical resistance of the regulator and the increased density of the breathing gases.
  - **oxygen toxicity** is not relevant in normal recreational diving on air to 50m (165 ft) where its partial pressure is only 1.2 atmospheres. It becomes very relevant when using enriched air or when being given 100% oxygen during recompression.

> **No other sport gives such a variety of stresses, so frequently, in such complex combinations and over such short time periods.**

The Physics

The basic physics of diving is always worthy of revision.

The pressure exerted on a diver

- The air (or atmospheric) pressure at sea level is one "atmosphere" (atm) of pressure.
- The water (or hydrostatic) pressure of 10 meters (33 feet) of sea water equals one atmosphere of pressure.
- The total (or absolute) pressure exerted on a diver is the sum of the air and water pressures. It is termed the atmospheric absolute (ATA).

Depth meters	Depth feet	Air pressure	Water pressure	Atmospheric Absolute pressure
Surface	Surface	1 atm	Nil	1 ATA
10	33	1 atm	1 atm	2 ATA
20	66	1 atm	2 atm	3 ATA
30	99	1 atm	3 atm	4 ATA
40	132	1 atm	4 atm	5 ATA
90	297	1 atm	9 atm	10 ATA

Pascal's Principle

Over the range of pressures encountered during sports scuba diving the liquid parts of the body are considered incompressible. Any pressure is transmitted through them with no distortion or damage to the tissues. Hence, water pressure pushes onto skin, which pushes onto fat, which pushes onto muscle, etc. with no distortion of those tissues.

However, the gas spaces in the body, namely the lungs, ears and sinuses, are compressible. These spaces will be squeezed by any increased pressure unless the air pressure inside them is also increased equally.

Boyle's Law

Boyle's Law states the volume of a gas is inversely proportional to its absolute pressure at *constant temperature*.

It is the gas law most relevant to sports diving.

Depth meters	feet	Absolute pressure in ATA	Relative volume
Surface	Surface	1	1
10	33	2	1/2
20	66	3	1/3
30	99	4	1/4
40	132	5	1/5
90	297	10	1/10

When absolute pressure is plotted against volume a curve is obtained (see graph) which demonstrates that the rate of change of volume is greatest the nearer the surface.

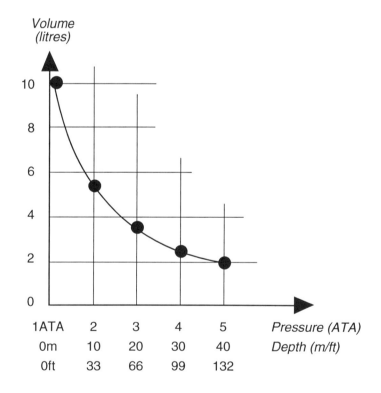

Relevance of Boyle's Law

Whenever the pressure within an air-containing cavity of the body differs from the surrounding pressure (the ambient pressure), the volume of that cavity will be subject to external "squeeze" in accordance with Boyle's Law. This usually involves damage to the surrounding tissues. The damage is called BAROTRAUMA, ie. trauma from pressure.

There are two main types of barotrauma:

Barotrauma of Descent

This will occur if, during descent, the external pressure becomes greater than the pressure within the air-containing cavity, eg. if the middle ear does not equalise as the diver descends.

In this case, the air space within the middle ear will be squeezed causing:
- stretching of the tympanic membrane into the middle ear until it perforates.
- oedema and haemorrhage of the mucosal lining of the middle ear and its orifices.
- accumulation of blood in the middle ear.

Barotrauma of Ascent

This will occur if, on ascent, the external pressure is less than the pressure within the air-containing cavity, eg. in the lungs as the scuba diver ascends and holds their breath.

In this event, the volume of the air within the lungs will expand until the pulmonary tissue is so overstretched it will tear at its weakest point. The expanding air from the lungs will then continue to follow the line of least resistance within the surrounding tissues and cause mediastinal emphysema and/or pneumothorax and/or enter the bloodstream causing arterial gas embolism (AGE).

The commonest forms of barotrauma seen in sports diving (in order of the author's experience) are:

barotrauma of the middle ear of descent (ear squeeze)

barotrauma of the sinuses of descent (sinus squeeze)

barotrauma of the sinuses of ascent

barotrauma of the middle ear of ascent

barotrauma of the external ear of descent (reverse ear squeeze)

barotrauma of the inner ear

barotrauma of the face (mask squeeze)

barotrauma of the lungs of ascent (burst lung/ pulmonary barotrauma)

Pulmonary barotrauma can develop with as little as $75 cmH_2O$ overpressure. It can occur and has occurred in a swimming pool.

As noted on the previous page, **the greatest pressure changes occur near the surface**. Most barotraumas occur within the first 10m (33ft) of depth. Therefore, if a diver is considered to be at risk from barotrauma, depth restriction is pointless.

Dalton's Law

Dalton's Law states that the total pressure exerted by a mixture of gases is the sum of the pressures that would be exerted by each of the gases if it alone occupied the total volume.

Air is a mixture of approximately 80% nitrogen and 20% oxygen.

Depth meters	Depth feet	Absolute pressure ATA	Partial pressure nitrogen ATA	Partial pressure oxygen (ATA)
Surface	Surface	1	0.8	0.2
10	33	2	1.6	0.4
20	66	3	2.4	0.6
30	99	4	3.2	0.8
40	132	5	4.0	1.0
90	297	10	8.0	2.0

Relevance of Dalton's Law

This law is very important in explaining the toxic effects of gases at depth, eg. nitrogen narcosis, carbon dioxide and carbon monoxide poisoning.

Nitrogen Narcosis is due to the narcotic effect of nitrogen when it is breathed at elevated pressures. This is commonly encountered at depths of 30m (100ft) or more when breathing air but it can occur at shallower depths. At 30m (100ft), the partial pressure of nitrogen is around 3.2 ATA.

The effects include impaired judgement, concentration and memory; sense of well being, lightheadedness and anxiety. As the partial pressure of nitrogen increases, symptoms will worsen, and, at extreme pressures, unconsciousness will occur. It is very similar to drunkenness. It is the most significant factor limiting the depth of safe sports diving (on air).

Diving factors such as mechanical resistance and dead space of the regulator, increased air density at depth, restriction of chest movement from equipment, exertion and slow breathing patterns can all contribute to higher than normal blood **carbon dioxide** levels. At depth, in accordance with Dalton's Law, the concentration of carbon dioxide can more easily reach toxic levels. Symptoms include headache, rapid breathing, dizziness, and confusion.

A 25 year old Australian male, an accomplished underwater photographer, did a dive to 60m (200ft) to photograph a huge gorgonia coral. Much to his horror all his photographs were poorly composed, underexposed and most were out of focus. He had not realised that he had been "narced".

Henry's Law

Henry's Law states that the amount of gas that will dissolve in a liquid is directly proportional to the partial pressure of that gas over the liquid at any given temperature.

Depth meters	Depth feet	Absolute pressure ATA	Approx. amount of nitrogen that will dissolve in a human body (litres)
Surface	Surface	1	1
10	33	2	2
20	66	3	3
30	99	4	4
40	132	5	5
90	297	10	10

Relevance of Henry's Law

This law is relevant to decompression sickness. The longer and deeper a dive, the greater the amount of nitrogen is absorbed. The time for nitrogen to fully equilibrate in the body is about 24 hours.

During a dive, extra nitrogen is dissolved into the body in accordance with Henry's Law. If decompression is too rapid, this extra nitrogen will come out of solution before it can be exhaled from the lungs. Decompression sickness is the term used for the effects of these nitrogen bubbles within the body.

The symptoms depend on the number and site of the bubbles and the local damage that the bubbles cause.

Common symptoms in sports divers include:

– pain of joints and muscles
– fatigue
– mental dullness
– paraesthesia
– numbness
– headache
– weakness
– dizziness and nausea.

The Divers

Divers can be divided into seven broad groups:

1. **RESORT DIVER**

   One who dives on a single day, under strict professional supervision, in optimal water conditions, according to an extremely conservative dive plan.

2. **RECREATIONAL or SPORTS DIVER**

   One who dives on air solely for pleasure and who can choose the time, place and plan for their diving.

3. **TECHNICAL DIVER**

   One who dives solely for pleasure but who pushes the limits of recreational diving to new frontiers, eg. deep penetration cave divers, deep divers using enriched air and other gas mixtures.

4. **PROFESSIONAL INSTRUCTIONAL DIVER**

   One who dives, usually on air, for employment in instruction and/or supervision of divers, eg. divemasters, diving supervisors, diving instructors.

5. **OCCUPATIONAL DIVER**

   (Not implying that they are not professional).

   One who dives, usually on air, for employment the nature of which determines the time, place and plan of the dive, eg. scientific diver, fish farm diver, abalone diver, police diver.

6. **COMMERCIAL DIVER**

   (Not implying that they are not professional or occupational).

   One who dives for employment using various gases and equipment, often involving hard manual work and in exacting conditions, eg harbour diving, oil rig divers.

7. **MILITARY DIVER**

   A law unto themselves but highly disciplined and sometimes diving in extreme circumstances.

The mental and physical demands on each class of diver differ considerably, and the medical standards for each must reflect those differences.

THIS BOOK IS ABOUT THE RECREATIONAL OR SPORTS DIVER.

The Sports or Recreational Diver

- In recreational diving, the degree of risk is decided by the diver. However, in commercial and professional diving, the degree of risk is determined by the job.

  The recreational diver may be at

  more risk because:
  - They receive less training.
  - Their diving has lower levels of supervision.
  - Their equipment is usually less well maintained.
  - There are usually less back-up facilities.
  - Dive planning is often less well prepared.
  - Dive profiles are usually shallower making barotrauma more likely.
  - They generally have less diving experience.
  - They commonly have long inactive periods from diving.
  - They often do not retrain or update their skills.
  - They are generally less physically fit.

  less risk because:
  - They can easily cancel or abort a dive.
  - They usually do not have to work hard whilst diving.
  - Whilst diving there is no urgency or pressure to "get a job done".
  - Their dive profiles are usually shallower and shorter, reducing risks of decompression sickness.

- Even amongst recreational divers the level of experience will affect the medical indications to pass or fail.

  The novice diver
  - Has little knowledge of the underwater environment and is unaware of the real risks involved.
  - Is often about to spend a large amount of money on a diving course or diving equipment.
  - Has few underwater skills (and often few general water skills!) so is more prone to buoyancy problems, fatigue, panic and uncontrolled ascents.

  The experienced diver
  - Knows the underwater environment and appreciates the real risks.
  - Has already obtained underwater skills.
  - Is often highly motivated and safety conscious (hence the repeat medical).

Why have a Diving Medical?

points to ponder

- The underwater environment is unfamiliar and unforgiving.
- Sports diving should be fun, not a source of morbidity or mortality.
- Sports diving is not a solo sport. On the contrary it is a SOCIAL sport. The majority of recreational divers dive with a buddy.
- Most recreational diving is organised as a club or commercially contrived group.
- A diver should feel confident that their buddy is adequately trained and medically fit.
- Neither the diving instructor nor the diver are medical experts capable of making an informed decision as to medical fitness to dive.
- Members of a diving group should feel confident that the other members are adequately trained and medically fit.
- Several dive buddies have been killed attempting to rescue their buddy.
- Many diving expeditions, especially in boats far off shore, have had to return to port with divers who became sick or injured because of pre-existing medical conditions, ruining the trip for fellow divers and causing unnecessary cost for the diving boat operator.
- Diving medical retrievals are very expensive.
- There are many medical conditions not compatible with safe diving.
- There are many medical conditions where diving may be recommended early in the course of the disease but where diving must be stopped as the disease progresses or relapses.
- Diving medical questionnaires alone only identify about HALF the divers who are not medically fit to dive.
- It is amazing how people forget or deny past major medical problems when filling out a questionnaire.
- A diving medical will include much advice on diving safety, eg equalisation of the middle ear, use of contact lenses underwater, smoking and diving.

BUT BEFORE YOU ASK . . ."
Why is a diver planning a "resort" or "introduction to diving" course not required to have a diving medical?

- Maybe they should.
- The resort diver has to fill in a questionnaire which should identify at least half of those not medically fit to dive.
- They only have one or two dives minimising their risk exposure (ie. they will probably get away with it).
- Water conditions must be perfectly calm with good visibility so minimising exercise demands and anxiety.
- Their dive plan is extremely conservative in time and depth, hopefully excluding decompression sickness.
- They are carefully watched and strictly supervised in order to promptly correct any minor problem before it develops into a major one or be quickly rescued should a major problem occur.
- Large numbers of people experience the underwater world in this manner to their great delight and education.
- There is no good evidence of increased morbidity or mortality in resort divers compared to other novice divers.

The Sports Diving Medical

This should consist of:

1. A questionnaire.
2. An interview with the diver to discuss the completed questionnaire.
3. A physical examination
4. Investigations.
5. Discussion and advice on findings of medical.

1. The QUESTIONNAIRE

See Table 1 for suggested format.

2. The INTERVIEW

This should expand and elucidate the positive answers given by the diver in the questionnaire. This book may help select further questions.

No matter what is marked on the questionnaire, experience shows divers often have "forgotten" or "did not think it important" to mark some questions. It is always worth verbally asking:-

a) Do you take any medications, medicines, pills or use inhalers of any sort? *Often the diver will admit to taking a pill which they did not think was important. Many women do not consider the contraceptive pill as a medication, and omit it.*

b) Have you ever had asthma or any breathing problems? *Some divers will mention wheezing attacks which they did not think significant.*

c) Have you ever smoked? *Many divers omit their smoking history once they have ceased smoking.*

d) Have you ever had any problems with your ears? *Even though recurrent ear infections are specifically asked about, many divers forget to include those acquired during childhood.*

Certain questions on the questionnaire promote useful discussion. The use of contact lenses and masks incorporating corrective lenses naturally follows the question on glasses. Ear pain in aircraft leads to discussion about Eustachian tube equalisation techniques. History of back pain requires lifting techniques to be reviewed.

QUESTIONNAIRE

Name _____ Sex _____

Address _____ DOB _____

_____ Age _____

Occupation_____ Nationality _____

Previous occupations _____

_____

Dive School_____

Would you rate your fitness: Excellent / Good / Fair / Poor (delete whichever not applicable)

	YES	NO
Do you have any disability or illness?		
Do you have a cold?		
Do you have a cough (smoker's or otherwise)?		
Are you suffering from hayfever?		
Is your hearing normal?		
Do you suffer from motion sickness?		
Do you take any pill, tablets, medication or any other drugs of any type?		
If yes please specify. _____		
Do you use an inhaler?		

Have you ever had or do you now suffer from any of the following?

	YES	NO		YES	NO
Asthma or wheezing?					
Pneumonia or Bronchitis?			Sinusitis, sinus pain or problems?		
Pleurisy?			Perforated ear drum?		
TB or consumption?			Discharge from the ear?		
Burst lung or pneumothorax?			Recurrent ear infections?		
Any operation on the chest or lung?			Operation on ears?		
Any other chest complaint?			Dizziness or vertigo?		
Do you smoke? How many?____			Deafness or difficulty in hearing?		
For how long? _____			Do you suffer ear pain in aircraft?		
Hayfever or blocked nose?			Any eye problems?		

	YES	NO		YES	NO
Do you wear glasses or contact lenses?			Have you ever been in contact with anyone with Tuberculosis (TB)?		
Heart attack or angina?			Are you pregnant?		
High blood pressure?			Any kidney or bladder disease?		
Stroke or cerebrovascular accident (CVA)?			Diabetes?		
			Any stomach or bowel disease?		
Palpitations?			Any liver disease?		
Any heart disease or abnormalities?			Are you late for your menstrual period?		
Depression?			Hernia?		
Panic attacks?			Any bleeding or blood disorder?		
Claustrophobia?			Any disease/disorder not listed?		
Any nervous disorders?			Have you ever had an operation?		
Epilepsy or fits?			Are you under the care of a doctor?		
Migraines or severe headaches?					
Head injury or concussion?			Have you ever snorkel dived?		
Paralysis or muscle weakness?			How many times?		
Bad back or back injury?			Have you ever scuba dived?		
Broken bones?			How many times?		
Any joint or bone disease?			Have you ever had an accident or problem whilst diving?		
Any skin disease?					

PLEASE NOTE: Although not compulsory, it is strongly recommended to have a routine chest X-ray before starting scuba diving as a full check for abnormalities of the lungs. Although rare, cysts can occur in the lung with no symptoms and could lead to a burst lung.

Do you wish to have a chest X-ray?_____YES/NO

I _____certify that all my statements are true and complete to the best of my knowledge.

Signed _____   Date _____

3. The EXAMINATION

This must be thorough and take special note of the air containing cavities of the body. The following is the author's routine and is included as a guide only.

Weight, height, body mass index and visual acuity are checked by a practice nurse.

Whilst patient sitting:

BLOOD PRESSURE – if high repeat in supine position.

PULSE – rate, rhythm and volume.

MOUTH – ?ulceration, ?palate deformities, ?bifid uvula, movement of soft palate(IX), ?gingivitis.

THROAT AND TONSILS – ?infection, ?post nasal discharge.

TEETH – ?caries, conditions of fillings, fitting of dental and orthodontic appliances.

NASAL PASSAGES – patency (get the diver to sniff through each nostril), ?septal deviation, ?polyps, ?discharge, mucosal colour.

EYES – presence of contact lenses, ?ptosis, pupillary reflexes to light and accommodation, eye movements (tests for cranial nerves III,IV,VI), ?nystagmus, fundi.

FACE – facial sensation with fine touch (V), screw up eyes and smile (VII), put out tongue (XII), rashes, eg. herpes simplex.

Diver stands up (it saves your back):

EARS

External ears – ?hearing aid, ?wax or debris (wash out or ear toilet required if unable to visualise the tympanic membrane), ?infection, ?exostoses.

Tympanic membrane – ?scarred, ?perforation, ?retraction, ?effusion, ?barotrauma, monomeric area (which `bulges like a balloon' when clearing the ear).

Eustachian tube function – it is important to try and observe movement of the tympanic membrane. For methods and notes on ear clearing see Appendix A.

Diver undresses and lies on couch:

NECK – ?cervical lymphadenopathy, ?enlarged thyroid, ?central trachea, ?increased jugular venous pressure, ?carotid bruits.

CARDIAC – ?apex beat displaced, ?thrills, heart sounds.

CHEST – shape or deformities, ?scars on chest wall from drains or surgery, ?normal respiratory movements, chest percussion, auscultatory sounds with both normal breathing and forced fast hyperventilation through an open mouth.

SPINE – ?deformities, ?overlying scars.

ABDOMEN – ?scars, ?splenic or hepatic enlargement, ?masses, hernial orifices, ?inguinal lymphadenopathy – listen for abdominal bruit in older divers.

PS – Routine examination of the genitalia is not indicated.

NERVOUS SYSTEM – Finger to nose, heel to shin coordination, all usual reflexes, muscle strength (can they walk on toes, heels, rise from squatting, arm and hand strength)

Skin sensation is asked for but not tested.

Pulses in feet.

Diver stands up and dresses:

SHARPENED ROMBERG BALANCE TEST or Tandem Romberg test – the author's method is for the diver to stand with their feet in a "heel to toe" position, fold their arms and close their eyes. Count how many times they stumble and start again before the diver can remain steady for 30 seconds. The average is 1-3 times. Record the longest time if unable to stabilise within 8-10 tries.

This manoeuvre narrows the proprioceptive base and places a severe strain on labyrinthine function. Alone it is not conclusive but should any diver be continually unable to stand for more than 15 seconds without falling they should be further examined neurologically in detail.

It can be recorded as the number of attempts and the longest time tested, eg. the diver has three attempts before balancing for 30 secs would be recorded a x3/30secs. A diver who keeps stumbling and only balances for 20 seconds even after 8 attempts would be recorded as x8/20secs.

GENERAL – During the examination specifically look for skin rashes, scars, muscle wasting and weakness, agility and mobility whilst getting undressed and climbing on and off the couch.

PSYCHIATRIC – Despite the brevity of a diving medical it is important to assess psychiatric state. Inappropriate comments or slightly unusual behaviour should be a warning. Jollying the diver along with friendly questions will often bring out further clues.

SERIAL SEVENS – Some doctors record a serial seven score as a base line for mental agility. It can be an aid in diagnosing decompression illness. The diver must subtract seven from a hundred and keep on subtracting seven from the answer.

100-93-86-79-72-65-58-51-44-37-30-23-16-9-2

Should any answer be wrong the doctor should correct it.

The number of mistakes and the time taken for a full sequence should be recorded. Hence a diver who takes 2 minutes and 10 seconds with six mistakes would be recorded as 6x/130secs. A diver who makes no mistakes and takes 32 secs would be recorded as 0x/32secs.

4. NORMAL INVESTIGATIONS

URINALYSIS – all divers should have their urine tested for protein and glucose.

LUNG FUNCTION – all divers should have spirometry to measure the forced vital capacity (FVC), forced expiratory volume in one second (FEV1) and their ratio FEV1/FVC. Normal predicted values should be calculated for age, sex and race. For a guide to lung function interpretation see appendix C.

AUDIOMETRY – air audiometry covering the frequencies 0.25Hz to 8Hz is recommended if there is a history, symptom or sign of hearing loss, middle or inner ear pathology. Many doctors would insist on a routine audiogram because divers damage their ears more than any other organ and it provides a baseline for future measurement.

CHEST X-RAY – a chest X-ray is recommended for any diver with:

- a personal medical history of serious or recurrent infection
- a personal medical history of a disease with possible respiratory complications
- a family history of tuberculosis
- a smoking history of ten pack years or more
- an occupational history with a high risk of lung disease
- previous medical history of mechanical ventilation of the lungs
- symptoms or signs of lung disease
- unexplained abnormal lung function tests

Many doctors would insist on a routine chest X-ray on all new divers.

It is recommended that all new divers be strongly advised to have a chest X-ray to exclude symptomless pulmonary conditions and cysts. The author incorporates this into his questionnaire (see Page 15).

TYMPANOGRAM – is recommended on any diver who cannot demonstrate autoinflation of their middle ear.

PREGNANCY TEST – is recommended for any female diver who is late for their menstrual period and could be pregnant. (Any woman trying to fall pregnant should be recommended not to dive).

ELECTROCARDIOGRAM (ECG) – an ECG is recommended for all male divers 45 years old or older or any female diver 55 years or older or any younger diver with numerous risk factors for coronary artery disease (viz. hypertension, smoking, obesity, increased cholesterol, family history) or any diver with cardiac symptoms who otherwise may be considered fit to dive, eg. a distant history of palpitations.

5. DISCUSSION

This should conclude the diving medical when the findings of the medical are revealed.

- Any medical condition that allows diving but could add a risk factor must be discussed and sensible precautions advised to reduce that risk, eg. extra decompression stops and slow ascent rates.
- Any reasons for failure must be fully explained. The failed candidate is often angry and resentful. This can be minimised by the examiner's patient explanations. Sometimes it cannot!
- Record all advice given to the diver on the diver's examination record.
- Any necessary investigation should be organised as quickly as possible.

A medical certificate should then be issued which includes:

- diver's full name
- date of medical
- type of diving medical (in this case a recreational diving medical)
- standard specification of medical if relevant (eg. AS4005.1 in Australia).
- whether passed, failed provisionally (and why) or failed permanently (and why).
- medical examiner's name, address, telephone number and signature.

A 22 year old male gave no significant past history on his questionnaire. At examination a small scar was noted on both sides of the chest wall suspiciously like those from a chest drain. When asked directly he admitted having had a motor bike accident the previous year in which he had sustained a crushed chest involving ten fractured ribs and bilateral pneumothoraces. He had been mechanically ventilated for three weeks and made a good recovery. He said that he had not mentioned it in the questionnaire because he did not think it important. Because of the extensive pleural adhesions and scarring to the lung tissue that must inevitably follow such an injury he was classed unfit to dive.

A 24 year old English male had travelled to Australia to learn to dive on the Great Barrier Reef. He had had a diving medical in England. Because he had a history of a ruptured ear drum after a water skiing fall four years previously his doctor had restricted his diving to 10m (33ft) maximum depth.

Examination showed his tympanic membranes to be completely normal and mobile and Eustachian tube function to be normal.

As the first 10m (33ft) of any dive is where the greatest rate of volume change occurs and the necessity to equalise the ears is the greatest, a depth restriction is illogical. The diver was therefore issued with a new diving medical certificate with no endorsements.

Repeat Diving Medicals

points to ponder

- The health of an individual changes and usually deteriorates with time.
- Many divers are allowed to dive in the early course of a disease but will need to stop diving prematurely as their disease progresses or relapses.
- It would seem sensible to have repeat diving medicals at frequent intervals.
- The intervals of medicals should vary with the class of diver and the diver's age.
- Professional and commercial divers all over the world have annual diving medicals by law.
- It would seem reasonable for a diver to have to show a current medical certificate for fitness to dive before joining a club or commercially organised diving trip.
- A suggested frequency for recreational sports diving medicals is every five years until 40 years of age and then every three years.
- Any diver with a medical condition that may deteriorate or relapse should be reviewed at least annually.
- Many divers have long periods without diving. A repeat diving medical is recommended before recommencing diving.
- A repeat diving medical should be advised after any major illness or after developing any new chest symptoms or shortness of breath.
- A chest X-ray should be obtained after any major chest complaint or injury and in heavy smokers.

A 38 year old Australian male came for a dive medical because he had not dived for ten years and wanted a check up before a proposed diving holiday. He felt well but had not had any regular exercise for five years. Examination revealed a BMI of 29, a BP of 170/110, an enlarged liver, glycosuria and a fine tremor. Investigation showed deranged liver function tests, a high fasting blood glucose and normal thyroid functions tests. After several months of diet, alcohol and caffeine restriction and an exercise program his weight, blood pressure, liver size and function, and blood glucose were all normal and he enjoyed his diving holiday the following year.

Endorsements

points to ponder

- Many doctors qualify "fitness to dive" by endorsing the medical certificate with a restriction.
- Recreational diving training agencies do not accept any endorsements. They consider that a candidate is either fit or not fit to undergo a diver training course.
- All training agencies include at least one dive to 18m (66 ft) in their basic scuba training course. Advanced courses often involve a dive to 30m (99 ft).
- On commercially organised recreational dives a diver does not have to show a valid medical certificate. Usually only a recognised qualification card is necessary.
- Endorsements therefore have little meaning and cannot be enforced.

  They should not therefore be used.

  It is more meaningful to discuss any potential problems with the diver and to recommend the limitations that they should self impose on their diving practices.
- The doctor should record ALL advice given to the diver on the diver's examination record.
- Common limitations that could be suggested may include:
  - additional safety decompression stops for divers with decompression sickness risk factors, eg. obesity, previous decompression sickness.
  - physically disabled divers to always dive with two buddies.
  - slow ascent rates, eg. 10m/min (33 ft/min) should be emphasised for heavy smokers.
  - to wear corrective lenses underwater (contact lenses or prescription masks) for divers with poor visual acuity.

A 15 year old Australian schoolboy had had a diving medical before coming on holiday to the Great Barrier Reef. He had passed but his doctor had endorsed his certificate with a 10m (33ft) diving restriction. The diving school could not accept the restriction as the PADI open water diving course involves dives to 18m (60ft). The risks and relevant points were discussed with the diver and his parents and a new certificate was issued with no depth restrictions.

General

AGE

- Most diving instructor organisations will teach divers from the age of 12 years with no upper age limit.

- Several Club Mediterranean villages run "mini scuba experiences" which have taken over 90,000 children between the ages of 4 to 12 years underwater with specially designed equipment to a depth of 1-2m (3-6ft) on a one to one basis with an instructor in continuous physical contact.

points to consider in young divers

- Children are not little adults.

- Mental maturity is essential to appreciate the dangers associated with scuba diving, especially pulmonary barotrauma of ascent and the discipline required for safe diving and emergency situations.

- Parental motivation for their children to dive should be assessed. Is the child being coerced to dive to comply with a parental demand for a family activity?

- The susceptibility of the epiphysis of rapidly growing bone to decompression sickness is completely unknown.

- The small build of children demands specially fitted equipment.

- Every diver in open water should be able to rescue their buddy.

- *The minimum age for open water diving courses is either 12 or 14 years, depending on the instructor body.*

- *Some diving doctors consider mental maturity of young teenagers to be insufficient and recommend a minimum age limit of 16 years.*

- *All children should always dive with an experienced and capable, adult diver.*

A 12 year old boy dropped an 88 cu ft tank on his leg whilst attempting to kit up at the poolside resulting in a fracture of his tibia. He was hardly able to lift it. Small people should have small equipment.

points to consider in older divers

- General physical condition and fitness usually deteriorates with age.

- There is a general acceptance of many medical conditions as "normal" in old age, eg. "arthritis".

- Existing medical conditions are more likely to be more advanced or "complicated" at an older age.

- Lung compliance reduces with age.

- Wisdom increases with age?

FITNESS

points to consider

- Physical fitness is one of the most important factors in scuba safety. Fatigue is a very important contributing factor to panic. Fit divers get fatigued less easily than unfit divers.

- Fitness for any activity is best tested by that activity itself, eg. fitness to snow ski is poorly tested by one's fitness to play tennis.

- It is important however to have a basic fitness. If any heavy exercise causes extreme distress diving should not be permitted until a fitness program has been undertaken.

- A simple test of basic fitness is the army's "physical fitness test". The diver is required to step at a rate of 30 times per minute to a height of 45 cm (18 inches) for five minutes. A standard sum of pulse counts taken for 30 seconds at 1, 2, and 3 minutes post exercise is made. The total should be less than 190.
  (A disadvantage of the test is that it relies on a relatively small muscle mass so local fatigue in the leg muscles alone could cause premature abandonment, especially in overweight divers. However finning, a purely leg activity, is very relevant whilst scuba diving).

- Alternatively, but less practical for the diving doctor, a test for basic fitness not reliant on one part of the body is to swim 200 metres (660 ft) unassisted within a 5 minute time period.

A 26 year old American male grid iron football player was 180cm (6ft 1in) tall and weighed 117kg (257lb) giving him a Body Mass Index (BMI) of 36. He was as wide as he was tall without an ounce of fat on his body. Not being intimidated by his threat to dislocate each of my limbs should I even think of failing him I conscientiously insisted on a fitness test which he completed without raising a sweat. He was classed fit to dive to whatever depth he chose.

SMOKING
Cigarettes

Cigarette smoking habits should be quantitated for a meaningful smoking history. This can be done by calculating the "pack-years", where a "pack-year" is the smoking of 20 cigarettes per day for one year. Hence

smoking 5 cigs/day for 8 years = 2 pack-years

smoking 40 cigs/day for 6 years = 12 pack-years

smoking 15 cigs/day for 4 years = 3 pack-years

points to consider

- Smoking causes an increase of mucus production in the nasopharynx and bronchial tree.
- Mucus plugs in the nasopharynx can block the Eustachian tube preventing equalisation of the middle ear.
- Mucus plugs in the bronchial tree have been well demonstrated to cause localised air trapping.
- Levels of carboxyhaemoglobin in smokers can be increased by at least 5% which could limit maximum exercise performance.
- Smokers have a higher incidence of acute and chronic respiratory infections.
- At post mortem 50% of smokers have emphysema.
- Most individuals with less than 25% of lung destroyed by emphysema are unaware of respiratory illness.

- *Any diver with a history of ten pack years or more should have a chest X-ray at their initial sports dive medical.*
- *All heavy smokers should have the potential dangers of smoking and diving fully explained and advised to be extra cautious in limiting their ascent rates to no faster than 10 meters (33 ft) per minute, especially near the surface.*

A 44 year old Australian male had smoked 60 cigarettes per day for 22 years, a total of 66 pack/years. He was quite healthy with normal lung function tests, chest X-ray and ECG. He was classed fit to dive but strongly advised to limit his ascent rate to 10m/min (33ft/min) and have regular dive medicals. It was suggested that his smoking should be at least moderated and preferably stopped and appropriate advice on methods given.

A 43 year old male gave a smoking history of 40/day for 20 years (ie. 40 pack-years). His lung function tests were normal but a routine chest X-ray showed a bulla in the right base and tenting of the hemidiaphragm. He was classed unfit to dive.

A 36 year old British male weighed in at 113kg (250lb). At a height of 175cm (5ft 9in) his Body Mass Index was calculated at 37. At examination he was obviously grossly obese. When given a fitness test he aborted after one minute and was happy to be classed as unfit to dive when informed scuba diving could be much harder work.

WEIGHT

A simple assessment of weight is to calculate the Body Mass Index (BMI).

$$BMI = \frac{\text{weight in kilograms}}{\text{height in meters}^2}$$

Hence a diver 180cm tall, 77kg in weight has a BMI

$$\frac{77}{1.8 \times 1.8} = \frac{77}{3.24} = 23.8$$

A diver 160cm tall and weighing 82kg has a BMI

$$\frac{82}{1.6 \times 1.6} = \frac{82}{2.56} = 32$$

A result of:

<20 = lean   20-25 = normal   26-30 = plump
31-35 = obese   35+ = grossly obese

This is only a guide and is not completely reliable since the very muscular body will have a high BMI. Hence a sensible clinical assessment should also be made.

points to consider in the underweight

- Consider and inquire about possible pathological causes, eg. anorexia, malnutrition, malabsorption.
- Equipment is more difficult to fit comfortably.
- There is a greater susceptibility to hypothermia.
- Reduced buoyancy will make overweighting more probable.

points to consider in the overweight

- General health and fitness are reduced with obesity.
- Specifically diabetes mellitus, hypertension and ischaemic heart disease are more common and cause premature death.
- Obesity may be a risk factor for decompression sickness.
- Increased buoyancy could make buoyancy control more difficult.
- There is a greater susceptibility to hyperthermia.
- Equipment is more difficult to fit comfortably.

- *Any diver with a BMI of 30 or greater should be warned that they have an extra risk factor for decompression sickness and extra safety factors should be included in their decompression planning.*
- *Any diver with a BMI greater than 35 should be very critically assessed for exercise tolerance.*

Cardiovascular System

The cardiovascular system can be subjected to numerous demands during scuba diving:

EXERCISE
- Can be strenuous and prolonged.
- Changes in exercise load can be sudden.

ANXIETY
- Will increase heart rate and blood pressure and cause hyperventilation

PANIC
- Severe acute anxiety reaction causing a massive sympathetic discharge resulting in very high rises in blood pressure and very high heart rates.
- Even if the panic is controlled, anyone with occult coronary artery disease could be severely compromised.
- Instead of a sympathetic activity one can have parasympathetic vagal response causing a slowing of the heart and dropping of the blood pressure (a typical faint).

COLD
- Will cause peripheral vasoconstriction and elevate blood pressure.
- Cold can occasionally provoke coronary artery spasm and angina.

DIVING REFLEX
- Caused by sudden immersion (especially of the face) in cold water which induces a sudden bradycardia and increase in blood pressure. Sometimes complicated by dysrhythmias.

HEAT
- Diving in tropical waters combined with heavy exercise can raise body temperature, reduce blood volume and blood pressure. (Alas a rarer problem!)

TOTAL BODY IMMERSION
- Will reduce the gravitational pooling of blood in the legs causing a shift of blood into the central circulation (which will cause a diuresis).

CORONARY ARTERY BYPASS SURGERY and CORONARY ANGIOPLASTY

points to consider very seriously

- Full details of the coronary artery disease and the surgery performed are needed to determine if bypassed lesions are isolated or part of widespread disease.

- *New divers with a history of coronary artery bypass surgery should be discouraged from diving.*
- *If asymptomatic, highly motivated novice and experienced divers should be considered in the same fashion as those who have had a myocardial infarct. (See Page 33.)*
- *There should not have been any pulmonary or neurological complications as a result of surgery.*

CORONARY ARTERY DISEASE
Angina
Ischemic heart disease

points to consider very seriously

- This causes many diving deaths, especially in the over 45 year olds.
- Usually due to atherosclerosis.
- Occult coronary artery disease is difficult to detect even with stress ECGs.
- Look for risk factors in the history, ie. little exercise, high BP, smoking, obesity, high cholesterol, diabetes.

- *Any male over 45 years of age or female over 55 years of age (or any diver with significant risk factors) should have an ECG.*
- *Diving is contraindicated in anyone with angina.*
- *Anyone with suspicious symptoms should be referred for a stress test and cardiological opinion.*

A 66 year old Spanish millionaire sailing along the Barrier Reef in his 24m (80ft) private yacht had a history of a triple coronary bypass 2 years previously. He had had no further chest pain, played tennis regularly but still smoked 20 cigarettes per day. Whilst diving alone at 22m (72ft) and finning against a current caused by the change in the tide he developed acute chest pain. He slowly ascended using his buoyancy compensator and was luckily spotted and rescued by another boat on the same reef. After evacuation a myocardial infarct was diagnosed and he made an uneventful recovery.

DYSRHYTHMIAS

points to consider very seriously

- Dysrhythmias reduce the efficiency of the pumping action of the heart and prevent normal responses of the heart to exercise.
- Immersion, cold, anxiety, exercise and hyperbaric conditions can all produce dysrhythmias.
- Diving can convert a minor dysrhythmia into a major one.
- Dysrhythmias have been strongly suggested as a cause of sudden death of divers.

Sinus Bradycardia

A pulse rate less than 60 per minute.

points to consider

- Commonly found in young people, especially athletes.
- To be considered normal the pulse rate should be seen to increase appropriately with exercise.
- Otherwise it will be associated with cardiac disease or drugs (eg. ß blockers and digoxin).

Sino atrial Disease
Sick sinus syndrome

points to consider very seriously

- Characterised by inappropriate bradycardia and episodes of sinus arrest.
- Increase liability of paroxysmal tachycardia.
- An important cause of syncope.
- *It is strongly recommended not to dive.*

Sinus tachycardia

A pulse rate greater than 100 per minute.

points to consider

- Can be caused by anxiety alone.
- Must exclude common causes, eg. fever, thyroid disease.
- *Diving is not recommended until the cause is determined and controlled.*

First degree heart block

A prolonged PR interval on the ECG.

points to consider

- Can be caused by a high vagal tone in young adults.
- However first degree heart block in the absence of some form of heart disease is unusual.
- *Anyone with first degree heart block, even with no obvious underlying cause, should have a full cardiological assessment for coronary artery disease before diving is considered.*

Second degree heart block and Circus reentry tachycardias
Mobitz type I
Mobitz type II
Wolf-Parkinson-White Syndrome
Lown-Ganong-Levine Syndrome

points to consider very seriously

- All will predispose to sudden paroxysmal dysrhythmias with the associated sudden limitation in exercise tolerance.
- *Diving is contraindicated.*

Third degree heart block

points to very consider very seriously

- Can be congenital.
- The commonest cause in the world is Chagas disease, (South American trypanosomiasis).
- May be associated with ischaemic heart disease especially in the "western world".
- The cardiac output cannot increase normally during exercise.
- *Most causes of third degree heart block will be a contraindication to diving.*
- *The heart block must be fully treated and stable before diving can ever be considered.*
- *A cardiological opinion must therefore be obtained.*

Paroxysmal Supraventricular Tachycardia
Paroxysmal atrial tachycardia

points to consider seriously

- Commonly the cause of palpitations in young people.
- Often associated with aggravating factors, eg. fatigue, alcohol, hunger, caffeine.
- *It is strongly recommended not to dive with a recent history or a history of recurrent palpitations.*
- *Any diver with any history of palpitations should first be evaluated by a cardiologist.*

Ventricular Ectopics
Extrasystoles
Premature beats

points to consider

- Normally cause no symptoms.
- Can give a sensation of an extra thump.
- Usually disappear as the heart rate increases.
- *If occasional and symptomless can be ignored.*
- *If frequent a cardiological opinion should be sought before diving is considered.*

A 50 year old Australian had a history of atrial fibrillation which had been successfully cardioverted eighteen months previously. He had been fully investigated by a cardiologist and no cause had been found. He was now asymptomatic and taking amiodarone prophylactically. Because of the cardiac dysrhythmic stimuli encountered underwater and the very serious consequences of a sudden reversion to atrial fibrillation whilst diving he was classed unfit to dive.

Right bundle branch block (RBBB)

points to consider

- Present in 0.5% of people under 50.
- If a solitary finding it is not normally associated with cardiac disease.
- If asymptomatic, less than 45 years of age with no CHD risk factors and a normal ECG, diving may be considered.
- *Otherwise a cardiological opinion and stress ECG should first be obtained.*

HYPERTENSION
High blood pressure

points to consider seriously

- Blood pressure tends to rise while diving due to cold, anxiety, exercise and the fluid shift from the legs.
- Long standing hypertension is associated with ischaemic heart disease and stroke. Both can incapacitate suddenly.
- Hypertension may predispose to pulmonary oedema whilst diving.
- Antihypertensive drugs commonly reduce the capability of the circulation to respond to stress and alter the response of the heart rate and blood pressure to exercise (and sometimes make males impotent!)
- ß blockers in particular may limit the cardiac response to exercise.

- *All divers should have a BP within normal range for age.*
- *Any diver found to have a high BP should be investigated and treated prior to diving.*
- *All known hypertensive divers should have fundi, ECG and renal function checked looking for end organ damage. If any of these are found it is stongly recommended not to dive.*
- *Anyone taking ß blockers is not recommended to dive until their exercise tolerance has first been evaluated.*
- *Anyone on moderate to high doses of antihypertensive drugs is strongly recommended not to dive.*
- *Hypertensive patients who do dive should have a medical every year.*

INTRACARDIAC SHUNTS

points to consider very seriously

- Intravenous bubbles commonly form in the circulation of sports divers on ascent.
- These bubbles are normally trapped in the pulmonary vascular bed and dissipated harmlessly.
- A diver who has an intracardiac shunt is at risk of paradoxical arterial gas embolism.

Septal Defects

Ventricular septal defects (VSD)
Atrial septal defects (ASD)

points to consider very seriously

- Both ASD and VSD are easily identified by their associated cardiac murmurs.
- There is usually right to left shunting of blood during the cardiac cycle.
- Any bubbles in the arterial circulation can embolise the central nervous system.

- *Anyone with an ASD or VSD is strongly recommended not to dive.*
- *Any diver with a suspected septal defect should have a full cardiological assessment with echocardiography before diving is considered.*

Repaired VSD, ASD

points to consider seriously

- The sternotomy scar does not involve pleural scarring.
- *Confirmation that the defect is fully closed and that there are no other associated abnormalities should be obtained from their cardiologist.*
- *Diving may then be considered.*
- *A chest X-ray should first be taken.*

A 28 year old American male had a history of asymptomatic congenital complete heart block which had been identified at a routine medical ten years previously. A variable rate pacemaker had been fitted. He was otherwise fit and he jogged everyday. Consultation with the pacemaker manufacturer confirmed pressure tolerance to 40 meters. After consultation with his cardiologist involving an exercise ECG he was classed fit to dive.

A 37 year old female was diving at 9m (30ft) on a "resort course". She became a little cold and anxious and suddenly felt faint and weak. Her instructor brought her to the surface and towed her to the nearby diving platform. She was found to have a pulse rate of 160/min. She was evacuated by air and admitted to hospital where her supraventricular tachycardia was treated. She later admitted having recurrent episodes but did not think it important when filling out her predive medical statement.

Patent Foramen Ovale (PFO)

points to consider very seriously

- The foramen ovale is the short circuit between the atria of the foetal heart which should close at birth by a flap mechanism which eventually seals.
- At post mortem up to 30% of normal hearts are noted to have incompletely sealed flaps, a PFO.
- These unsealed flaps/valves can open, especially during a Valsalva manoeuvre.
- Studies have suggested that divers suffering severe decompression sickness have a higher incidence of PFO.
- It has been suggested that all divers should be screened for PFO by echocardiography.
- It has also been suggested that all divers should at least have the statistics and potential dangers of PFO explained to them so that they might make an "informed decision" as to whether to dive.

- *Any diver who knows that they have a PFO must be informed that it could be a risk factor for decompression sickness. If they do decide to dive they should be advised to avoid decompression stop diving, ascend no faster than 10m/min (33 ft/min) and always include a short safety decompression stop at 5-6m (15-20 ft) on all dives.*

Persistent Ductus Arteriosus

points to consider

- Small shunts can be asymptomatic.
- Causes a continuous machinery murmur.
- The shunt is always left to right and does not change with a Valsalva manoeuvre unless there is pulmonary hypertension.
- All such shunts are surgically closed to remove the risks of bacterial endocarditis.
- *If surgically ligated, diving may be considered if the surgical approach was through a sternotomy scar.*
- *If not repaired, a cardiological opinion should first be obtained.*

32

MYOCARDIAL INFARCT
Heart attack
MI

points to consider very seriously

- Usually indicative of serious ischaemic heart disease.
- The site of the infarct is prognostically significant.

■ *Any new diver who has had an MI should be strongly discouraged from diving.*

■ *An experienced, or very highly motivated new diver must*
  - *have no complications*
  - *be asymptomatic*
  - *have a normal stress ECG or preferably a normal coronary artery angiogram*
  - *a delay of at least a year post infarct*
  - *have completed a supervised exercise program for several weeks prior to diving*
  - *adhere to a program of risk factor control (abstain from smoking, control weight, lipids and blood pressure).*
  - *dive only with other experienced and informed divers.*
  - *the diving should not be too strenuous and in sheltered waters (and preferably warm water).*
  - *have annual dive medicals but should symptoms recur between medicals, the diver must cease diving until reviewed.*

PACEMAKERS

points to consider seriously

- The reason why a pacemaker is fitted will normally disqualify the wearer (eg. heartblock, sick sinus syndrome).
- Many pacemakers are designed to withstand pressures up to 4 ATA or greater, but some will only withstand 2 ATA pressure.
- Fixed rate pacemakers will not allow adequate exercise tolerance.
- Sequential pacemakers allow normal cardiac response to exercise.

■ *Most divers requiring pacemakers will be disqualified by their underlying pathology that requires the pacemaker.*

■ *Any benign cause (eg. congenital heart block) which is treated with a pacemaker should have a cardiological assessment prior to diving.*

■ *It is essential to check the pressure tolerance of each individual pacemaker with the manufacturer's specification.*

PERIPHERAL VASCULAR DISEASE

points to consider very seriously

- Nearly always coexists with coronary artery disease and often cerebral vascular disease.
- Often associated with diabetes and heavy smoking.
- Exercise tolerance may be limited by intermittent claudication.
- Symptoms will be exacerbated by cold.

■ *It is strongly recommended not to dive, even if asymptomatic.*

RAYNAUD'S PHENOMENON

Spasmodic contraction of the digital arteries.

points to consider seriously

- Can be secondary to connective tissue disorders, obliterative arterial disease, occupations where the hands are exposed to vibration, cold agglutinins and cryoglobulins.
- Often aggravated by cold and emotion.
- Can result in thrombosis and ischaemic changes in the skin of the digits and nails.

■ *If primary, the diver should be warned of the possible consequences and of the importance of keeping not only the hands warm by using thermal protection, but the whole body.*

■ *If secondary, the implications of the primary condition must first be assessed.*

A 36 year old Australian female had a history of recurrent Raynaud's phenomenon. The previous year she had suffered swollen cyanotic fingers requiring hospitalisation where she had been given felodipine, a calcium channel antagonist which had settled her symptoms. Investigations for an underlying pathology had been normal. It was explained to her that as cold is the classic provocative agent she was risking recurrence by diving and she was happy to be classed as unfit.

A 45 year old American male had a history of an inferior myocardial infarction 2 years previously. He had dived previously and had logged 300 dives. He now walked 3km (2miles) daily and had given up smoking. However he was still overweight (BMI=32) and his blood pressure was 160/90 despite taking enalapril 5mg daily. In view of his history and two remaining risk factors for coronary artery disease he was classed unfit to dive. He was advised that if he lost weight to bring his BMI to normal he could then be considered for diving.

An elderly American couple accompanying their diving son, went snorkelling from the dive boat. They were given wetsuits to wear. Whilst waiting for his wife, who was very slow to get ready, the man stood in the hot sun for nearly half an hour. He suddenly collapsed with chest pain and was urgently evacuated. Investigation confirmed a myocardial infarct thought to be aggravated by heat stroke.

VALVULAR HEART DISEASE

A. Regurgitation

Mitral regurgitation

Aortic regurgitation

Tricuspid regurgitation

Pulmonary regurgitation

points to consider very seriously

- Small abnormalities of the valves can be tolerated very well.

- Regurgitation could be aggravated if the systematic vascular resistance is increased by immersion and diving equipment (eg. a tight wet suit).

- Large abnormalities will cause a large volume overload on the heart which when combined with the volume shift from the legs (with immersion) and heavy exercise (increasing cardiac output) can result in cardiac failure.

- *Ask about exercise tolerance (eg. sporting activities in daily life).*
    - *If poor or inactive, they should be assessed by a cardiologist (including an echocardiogram).*
    - *If active and undertaking regular exercise, diving may be considered after an ECG to exclude ventricular hypertrophy.*

B. Stenosis

Aortic stenosis

Mitral stenosis

Tricuspid stenosis

Pulmonary stenosis

points to consider very seriously

- The stenotic valve causes obstruction to flow of blood through the heart.

- High pressure gradients can form across the stenotic valve.

- Aortic stenosis can present as sudden death during exercise.

- *Any known or suspected valve stenosis should be fully assessed by a cardiologist (including an echocardiogram) before diving is considered.*

Mitral valve Prolapse

Barlow's syndrome

Floppy mitral value syndrome

points to consider seriously

- Occurs in 5% of males and 10% of females (a normal variant?).

- Causes a midsystolic click and late systolic murmur.

- The amount of regurgitation is usually very small and of no consequence.

- Can cause chest pain, palpitations, dysrhythmias and syncope.

- *Any diver with any associated symptom is strongly recommended not to dive.*

- *If asymptomatic diving can be considered.*

CARDIAC VALVE PROSTHESES

points to consider very seriously

- The presence of other serious cardiac pathology must be assessed.
- By-pass surgery commonly involves neurological and pulmonary complications.
- There may be a significant pressure gradient across the prosthetic valve in high output states (eg. during exercise) interfering with valve opening.
- Most patients with prosthetic valves are anticoagulated with all the inherent risks. (See under anticoagulants on Page 47).
- Embolisation from the left heart could cause unconsciousness or neurological symptoms similar to diving-related diseases.
- Left heart valves occasionally fail (approx 1-2 per 1000 years) with catastrophic results.

- *It is strongly recommended not to dive.*

VARICOSE VEINS

points to consider

- Varicose veins will bleed profusely if traumatised.
- Short legged wet suits can constrict the upper leg causing engorgement of the veins in the legs.

- *It is recommended that varicose veins are protected and supported by a long legged wet suit or elastic stocking whilst diving.*

A 53 year old Israeli female was diving in a short legged wet suit and was severely overweighted. Whilst diving she lacerated her right leg on the coral severing a large varicose vein which bled profusely. By the time she reached the dive boat she had suffered significant blood loss which was quickly controlled with compression and elevation.

Connective Tissue and Rheumatic Diseases

points to ponder

- They are multisystem diseases.
- There may be relapses and remissions lasting months to years.
- With such diseases it is often difficult to maintain physical fitness.

ANKYLOSIS SPONDYLITIS
Sacroiliitis

points to consider seriously

- The onset is usually insidious.
- Intrinsic lung disease is rare (1.3%).
- Limitation of ventilation can occur through involvement of the costovertebral joints.
- Extra-articular features include aortic regurgitation, cardiac conduction defects, apical pulmonary fibrosis, osteoporosis, myelopathy associated with atlanto-axial subluxation.

- *Diving may be considered in mild cases but should be first referred to a rheumatologist for full assessment.*
- *It is strongly recommended not to dive for those with active inflammatory spinal disease; or who have significant restriction of neck, spine or chest; or evidence of any extra-articular complication.*

"ARTHRITIS"
eg. Gout
  pseudogout
  osteoarthritis
  psoriatic arthritis

points to consider

- All arthritic disease involves joint pains.
- Many patients suffer intermittent mild joint pains or "twinges". Any diver with such a history may easily explain any joint pain following a dive by their illness.
- It has been suggested that a joint damaged by "arthritis" is more susceptible to decompression sickness.
- Joints which are acutely inflamed or chronically damaged will limit both general mobility and fine movements, interfering with adjustment of equipment.

- *Any diver with an acutely inflamed joint or poor agility is strongly recommended not to dive.*
- *Any diver with a history of arthritis should avoid decompression stop diving, deep diving and repetitive diving since such diving practices appear to increase the risk of decompression sickness.*

RHEUMATOID ARTHRITIS

points to consider seriously

- Rheumatoid arthritis is not just an "arthritis" but a systemic disease where the joints give most of the symptoms.
- General weakness and easy fatigue are common symptoms.
- Gross weakness of grip could compromise fine hand movements, eg. buoyancy compensator control, weight belt release.
- Joint destruction and deformity may limit mobility.
- Involvement of the cervical spine may cause atlanto-axial subluxation.
- Pulmonary disease uncommonly precedes joint symptoms by several years.
- Lung involvement is clinically uncommon but pleuritis is very commonly found in autopsy.
- Lung involvement may include asymptomatic pleural effusion, pulmonary fibrosis or rheumatoid nodules in the lung parenchyma.
- Constrictive pericarditis can occur with few if any symptoms until prolonged exercise demands a higher cardiac output.
- Muscle wasting may cause significant weakness.
- "Rheumatoid ear" has been described with related stiffness of the tympanic membrane and ossicles which theoretically could predispose to aural barotrauma.

- *Diving should only be considered in mild cases in remission. Lung function tests should be within normal limits and a chest X-ray should be taken.*

A 35 year old Canadian male had a 15 year history of rheumatoid arthritis. He had been on gold injections but one year previously he had commenced methotrexate. His condition had stabilised and his only complaint was mild pain and effusion in his left knee. He had had a cortisone injection into the joint a month previously. His respiratory functions tests were completely normal, his chest X-ray was clear and he was fully mobile. He was classed fit to dive but strongly advised to have annual medicals and to stop diving should his condition suddenly deteriorate. He was also warned that any joint pains after diving could be due to decompression sickness and not his arthritis so he should dive very conservatively.

SYSTEMIC LUPUS ERYTHEMATOSUS (SLE),
Disseminated lupus erythematosus (DLE)

A multisystem connective tissue disease.

points to consider very seriously

- Symptoms include Raynaud's phenomena, pericarditis, fibrosing alveolitis, "shrinking lung syndrome".
- Pleuropulmonary disease is present in 50% of patients.
- Common pulmonary manifestations include pleuritis and atelectasis.
- *Diving is not recommended even in mild cases.*

SCLERODERMA
Progressive systemic sclerosis. CRST or CREST syndromes.

points to consider very seriously

- Severe Raynaud's phenomena is usually the presenting symptom.
- Pulmonary fibrosis occurs in most cases.
- Loss of lower oesophageal peristalsis predisposes to gastric reflux.
- Other problems include cardiomyopathy, heart block and aortic valve lesions.
- *Diving is not recommended, even in mild cases.*

An obese 37 year old Australian male was rushed back to the mainland following a dive because he had the 'bends'. He complained of excruciating pain in his left foot which began 30 minutes after a dive. Examination demonstrated a swollen, erythematous and very tender first metatarsal-phalangeal joint. He was reassured that he did not have decompression sickness and treated for his gout.

Dental

- The mouth is an important organ in diving. It holds the regulator, which should be positioned securely and comfortably.
- The teeth can be subject to barotrauma of both descent and ascent.
- Gas can enter any break in the mucosa of the mouth and track into the tissues, eg. after oral surgery.

CARIES

points to consider

- A carious tooth containing a cavity can implode as the wall of the cavity collapses on descent.
- A carious tooth can allow air into a cavity on descent. Subsequent rapid ascent can cause toothache or explosion of the tooth as trapped gas expands but cannot escape.
- Carious tooth sockets are often infected.
- *All caries should be treated before diving.*

DENTAL FILLINGS

points to consider

- Cracked fillings can allow gas into the filling on descent. Subsequent rapid ascent can cause acute toothache or even explosion of the filling as trapped gas expands but cannot escape.
- Incomplete root canal treatment with temporary fillings and possible air spaces can also cause toothache.
- Underwater welding can cause a metallic taste and erosion of the filling in divers with metallic fillings.
- *All divers should have regular dental check-ups.*
- *Diving is not recommended for 24 hours after dental procedures.*

An 18 year old Dane was doing his first ocean dive to 15m (49ft). At 12m (39ft) depth he felt a sharp pain in his left upper jaw. It was so severe he had to abort the dive. A molar had imploded on a cavity along-side a faulty filling.

A 30 year old Irish male was seen to have a mouthful of carious teeth with an associated gingivitis and halitosis. He was proposing to commence a diving course the next day. He was classed unfit to dive because his poor oral hygiene could cause a risk of cross infection whilst buddy breathing and he would be at risk of dental barotrauma.

DENTAL EXTRACTIONS

point to consider

- Whilst diving, gas can track through the broken oral mucosa and into the tissues.

  ■ *Diving is not recommended until healing of the gums is complete. A minimum of two weeks is recommended.*

DENTURES

points to consider

- The regulator must be secure in the mouth.
- A small partial denture is difficult to adjust with a regulator in the mouth.
- A partial denture can easily be lost during a rescue and emergency resuscitation.

  ■ *Full dentures should be firm fitting.*
  ■ *Partial dentures should be clasped.*

MOUTH ULCERS

points to consider

- Consider the underlying cause of the ulcer, eg. infective, herpetic, neutropenia, aphthous.
- Holding a regulator in the mouth for prolonged periods may be uncomfortable and aggravate the ulcerative condition.

ORTHODONTIC APPLIANCES

point to consider

- Scuba regulator mouthpieces can irritate such appliances.

  ■ *Custom made scuba mouthpieces are recommended.*

PERIODONTAL DISEASE

point to consider

- In advanced disease, gum retraction and loose teeth occur.

A 22 year old female had had a dental extraction three days before she undertook a resort course. During her dive she felt her gums swelling. By the time she surfaced the right side of her jaw and cheek were very swollen with obvious crepitus. She was rushed to a medical clinic suspected of an air embolism!

A 34 year old male jumped into the water and swallowed his partial denture as it became dislodged. A subsequent X-ray confirmed its presence in the stomach and it was passed per rectum two days later.

Dermatology

points to ponder

- The skin is commonly subject to numerous insults whilst diving.
    - **chafing** especially by swimwear, wet or dry suit, mask and fins.
    - **prolonged immersion** will cause skin maceration.
    - **minor abrasions and lacerations** from equipment and underwater terrain.
    - **stings** from marine animals and plants.
    - **urine irritation** due to an induced diuresis, lack of bladder capacity or just a warming technique!
    - **salt** which is hydrophilic and abrasive.
- Suit squeeze (in dry suits) can subject the skin to negative pressures.
- Compressed air on broken skin can track into the subcutaneous tissues and cause swelling and pain.

BURNS

point to consider

- Prolonged immersion in sea water will both delay healing and predispose to infection.

COLD URTICARIA
Acquired cold urticaria (ACU) syndrome

points to consider very seriously

- Every diver gets cold.
- 70% of patients with cold urticaria have systemic symptoms.
- 38% have hypotension.
- Syncope is not uncommon.
- The commonest aggravating cause is aquatic activity.
- A quick test of activity is to apply an ice-filled bag to the forearm and note the time needed for a coalescent weal to form. A time of less than three minutes indicates a severe reaction.

- *Diving is not recommended, even in apparently mild cases.*

A 44 year old female with a known history of cold urticaria went swimming in the tropics believing that the warm tropical waters were safe. After twenty minutes in the water she felt very faint, but managed to summon help and was towed to safety. When examined she was found to be hypotensive and to have a widespread urticarial rash. She was advised not to dive again.

CONTACT SKIN ALLERGY
Allergic dermatitis
Contact dermatitis

points to consider

- Skin allergy to rubber (often the anti-oxidant IPPDA) can cause allergic dermatitis from the use of rubber masks, mouthpieces, unlined neoprene wet suits, nose clips, fins and fin straps.

- Contact dermatitis can be caused from a thiourea compound used to cement the nylon lining to the rubber suit, similar to the one that produced "Nike sneaker dermatitis".

- The dermatitis can occur 8-48 hrs after exposure.

- Masks and mouthpieces made of silicone rubber are virtually hypoallergenic.

- *Equipment that is free of the offending allergen should be sought and tested before diving.*

CORAL CUTS

points of interest

- The smallest scratch from coral can readily become infected, especially in tropical climates.

- Subsequent diving and marine activities will predispose to skin maceration and further contamination.

- Nematocysts and coral slime may cause an early tissue reaction with itching and stinging.

- Infection may occur from either skin organisms or marine bacteria.

- Foreign body reactions from implanted coral fragments may occur.

- Even with thorough first aid, many coral cuts will cause severe cellulitis.

- *Any small abrasion acquired before or during diving must receive adequate first aid after every dive, namely:*
  - remove all foreign bodies and thoroughly clean by scrubbing in warm water (each diver should have their own small scrubbing brush, eg. a soft toothbrush, to avoid cross infection between divers).
  - clean with an antiseptic, eg. chlorhexidine or povidone-iodine 10%.
  - apply an antibiotic ointment, eg. mupirocin.
  - Should cellulitis occur, treatment with oral antibiotics, doxycyclin or cotrim, should be commenced.
- *All divers should ensure their tetanus vaccination is current (a booster within the last ten years).*

43

DERMATITIS

points to consider

- Prolonged immersion will cause skin maceration and predispose any area of dermatitis to infection.

- *Any diver with areas of dermatitis should keep the area as dry as possible between dives and use an antibiotic ointment to treat any infection should it occur.*

- *Any diver with a large expanse of dermatitis should delay diving until it has settled.*

DIVER'S GREEN HAIR

point of interest

- A greenish discolouration of the scalp hair of blonde divers after using swimming pools treated with copper algaecide solutions.

FACIAL CUTS

point to consider

- Recent lacerations of the skin on the face within the mask area may allow air to enter the subcutaneous tissues and cause subcutaneous emphysema on ascent.

- *Diving should be postponed for at least a week after any facial laceration within the mask area.*

HERPES SIMPLEX ON FACE
Cold sores

points to consider

- Herpes simplex can be aggravated by sunlight.
- The common lip lesion can extend over the cheek and under the mask seal causing severe irritation.
- The lip lesion can be irritated by the mouthpiece of the regulator.

- *Shared regulators and masks need to be cleaned and disinfected between divers.*

PHOTOSENSITIVITY OF THE FACE

points to consider

- Many drugs increase the sensitivity of the skin to sunlight which is then more prone to sunburn.

- *Extra precautions against sunburn should be undertaken, especially wearing a hat when not in the water, wearing a shirt when not in a wetsuit and regularly replenishing a 15+ sunscreen on all exposed skin.*

A 32 year old Canadian female theatre nursing sister had a history of anaphylaxis to latex rubber. She had researched the content of latex rubber in hospital equipment and enquired about its use in diving equipment. The only use of latex rubber was found in some brands of regulator mouthpieces. These she avoided and dived uneventfully during her course.

SCARRING OF FACE

point to consider

- Severe scarring of the face, eg. burns, can interfere with the seal of a mask.

SKIN INFECTIONS

Bacterial eg. impetigo
Fungal eg. tinea

point to consider

- Prolonged immersion, humid environments and chafing will all aggravate existing skin infections and delay healing.

SUNBURN

point of interest

- One of the commonest problems that spoils diving enjoyment in the tropics.

- *Any diver proposing to go to a warm climate to dive should be advised how to avoid sunburn; namely:*

  - *wear a hat whenever in the sun*
  - *wear a shirt whenever in the sun*
  - *apply 15+ sunscreen several times a day, especially after diving*
  - *only expose the skin to short periods (initially 10-20 mins) of sunlight if sunbaking, especially during the peak ultra violet periods of the day, 10am to 2pm.*

A 24 year old British male was cruising out to the Great Barrier Reef to complete his open water dives for his diving certificate. During the cruise he fell asleep whilst sun baking on the upper deck for over an hour and suffered severe sunburn to 49% of his body! He was evacuated by seaplane to the mainland in considerable pain and was unable to complete his dive course.

A 45 year old male scratched his ankle on coral during a dive. He cleaned it with soap and water in the shower and applied antiseptic cream. Despite this adequate first aid the ankle became red, swollen and very painful. He initially ignored the infection but the following day his lower leg was grossly oedematous, erythematous and extremely painful. He was admitted to hospital for limb elevation and antibiotic treatment and was able to be discharged five days later.

Drugs

points to ponder

- What is the underlying reason to take the drugs? Does the condition disqualify from diving?
- What are the side effects of the drug at atmospheric pressure, eg. sedation, nausea and vomiting?
- Will these side effects cause danger in the underwater environment?
- Are there any possible drug interactions?
- Side effects of drugs may be confused with symptoms of decompression illness.
- Will the side effects be enhanced by hyperbaric conditions, nitrogen narcosis, carbon dioxide toxicity, cold or fatigue?
- Will new side effects occur because of hyperbaric conditions, nitrogen narcosis, carbon dioxide toxicity, cold or fatigue?
- The effects of drugs varies widely between individuals.
- Over 40 drugs have been associated with pulmonary toxicity.
- There has been very little research into the side effects of drugs in the 2-5 ATA pressure range.
- The safe use of most drugs in diving has not been established.
- Seasickness can interfere with drug taking and absorption.
- *No diver should dive if they have recently commenced taking a new drug until they are confident the drug is not causing any compromising side effects.*

ALCOHOL

points to consider very seriously

- Causes depression of the central nervous system reducing judgement, coordination and reaction time.
- Nitrogen narcosis can be enhanced.
- Gastric irritation can cause vomiting.
- Peripheral dilation accelerates heat loss and hypotension.
- The associated diuresis could cause dehydration and aggravate decompression sickness.
- Chronic alcohol abuse damages the liver, heart and brain.
- *No alcohol should be taken for at least eight hours prior to diving.*
- *No diver should drink large amounts of alcohol the night before a dive.*
- *Drink plenty of water after drinking alcohol and before diving.*

ANALGESICS
Pain killers

points to consider seriously

- The reason for taking the analgesic is most important. Anyone with an acute pain (eg. tension headache or hangover) should delay diving until better. Anyone in chronic pain, such as a back injury, should not be diving.
- Mild analgesics are relatively safe but due to the possible anti-coagulant effects of aspirin, paracetamol is advised.
- Stronger analgesics containing codeine or dextro-propoxyphene can have sedative side effects and enhance the effects of nitrogen narcosis.
- Narcotic analgesia reflects a serious underlying medical condition or addiction and has strong sedative side effects.

- *Any diver with chronic or disabling pain is strongly recommended not to dive.*
- *No analgesic should be taken at least 24 hours before a dive, except paracetamol for minor conditions.*

ANTIBIOTICS

points to consider

- Consider whether the reason to take the antibiotic is disqualifying.
- Nausea is a common side effect of many antibiotics.

- *As long as the reason for taking the antibiotic is not disqualifying, diving may be considered.*

ANTICOAGULANTS
**eg. Warfarin
Phenindione
Low dose aspirin**

points to consider very seriously

- Barotrauma is a common injury during diving which often causes bleeding in the air-containing cavities of the body, eg. middle ear, sinus and lung.
- Minor skin trauma is common during diving, eg. abrasions, small lacerations.
- An increased bleeding time will seriously complicate minor trauma.
- Neurological decompression sickness (especially in the spinal cord) may involve haemorrhage into the neural tissue.

- *It is strongly recommended not to dive.*

A 54 year old Australian male had a history of a deep vein thrombosis three months previously and was taking warfarin. A PTT two weeks earlier had shown a ratio of 2.8. He went on a dive to 15m (50ft) for 40 mins. When he saw a small shark he made a fast ascent. Shortly afterwards he began coughing up blood stained sputum, more blood than sputum. He had no pain or breathlessness or neurological symptom or sign. His chest X-ray was clear. He was admitted to hospital and given 100% oxygen for six hours. His haemoptysis stopped the next day and he was discharged. He was classified as a probable pulmonary barotrauma aggravated by his anticoagulated status. He was strongly recommended not to dive whilst taking anticoagulants and to have a full diving medical assessment before diving again.

ANTI-CONVULSANTS
eg. Phenytoin
Carbamazepine

points to consider very seriously

- Common side effects include sedation, dizziness, ataxia and reduced concentration.
- Nitrogen narcosis may be enhanced.

▪ *If taken for the control of epileptic convulsions, diving is contraindicated.*

▪ *Even if not taken for convulsions, it is strongly recommended not to dive.*

ANTI-CHOLINERGICS
eg. Hyoscyamine

points to consider

- Used as an anti-spasmodic.
- Common side effects include dryness of mouth and tachycardia.
- Reduction in sweating could contribute to hyperthermia in hot climates.

ANTI-DEPRESSSANTS

points to consider very seriously

- Both tricyclic and monoamine oxidase inhibitors commonly cause drowsiness, dizziness, dry mouth, weakness, fatigue and hypotension.
- Some anti-depressants can cause cardiac dysrhythmias.

▪ *It is strongly recommended not to dive.*

ANTIEMETICS
Hyoscine
eg. Kwells,
Scop patches

points to consider

- Commonly used by divers against seasickness.
- Can cause drowsiness.
- Less commonly causes impairment of memory and concentration, restlessness, dizziness, disorientation and confusion.
- Should not be combined with alcohol.

▪ *Limited studies indicate that it is probably safe to use as prophylaxis against seasickness in recreational diving.*

▪ *Remind divers to wash their hands after applying Scop patches otherwise hand contamination of the eye could cause prolonged dilation of the pupil.*

▪ *Divers should check for individual side effects by first taking on days when not diving.*

A 20 year old Australian male, on a night dive, ascended under a dingy hitting his head and causing a severe laceration which bled profusely. When attended he was drowsy but easily rousable. He smelt heavily of alcohol and his friends confirmed he had drunk over half a bottle of wine with dinner. His laceration was sutured and he was admitted for head injury observation overnight. His alcohol intake probably accounted for the carelessness on his ascent.

Phenothiazines
eg. Prochlorperazine

points to consider

- Consider the reason for their use.
- Not very effective for seasickness.
- Can cause drowsiness and restlessness.
- Can rarely cause dystonic extrapyramidal reactions.

■ *Diving is not recommended.*

Metochlopramide

points to consider

- Consider the reason for their use.
- Not very effective for seasickness.
- Can cause drowsiness, restlessness, fatigue and lassitude.
- Dystonic extrapyramidal reactions can rarely occur.

■ *Diving is not recommended.*

ANTI-HYPERTENSIVES

points to consider very seriously

- All drugs used for hypertension affect the autonomic nervous system.
- Side effects such as impotence, loss of libido, flushing, fainting, paraesthesia, constipation may not all be relevant to diving but demonstrate the disruption of normal bodily function.

ß Blockers
eg. Atenolol, Propanolol

- Exacerbate bronchospasm and allergic rhinitis in atopic people.
- Normally cause bradycardia and a reduced cardiac exercise response.
- Frequently cause fatigue and dizziness.

■ *ß blockers should only be given in low dosage, eg. 25-50mg atenolol. Alternative drugs should be used if higher dosages are required.*

■ *Ensure an appropriate cardiac response to exercise.*

(Topical Eye Drops
eg. Timolol)

Eye drops used for glaucoma can be absorbed systemically and rarely could cause side effects as above.

■ *Systemic absorption of eye drops can be reduced (and absorption into the eye can be increased) by gentle compression of the lacrimal punctate for two minutes after instillation of the drops into the lower conjunctival sac.*

Peripheral Vasodilators
eg. Prazosin, Calcium ion Antagonists

- Common side effects include postural hypotension, palpitations, drowsiness and weakness.
- Being vasodilatory they can increase heat loss.

A.C.E. inhibitors
eg. Captopril

- Common side effects include hypotension. They can also cause fatigue, dizziness and bronchospasm.
- A persistent cough due to increased bronchial reactivity can develop.

Methyldopa

- Side effects include sedation, headache, weakness, postural hypotension, nasal stuffiness. Bradycardia can occur.

- *Any diver on moderate to high doses of antihypertensive drugs is strongly recommended not to dive.*
- *Any diver on small doses of antihypertensive drugs should have an exercise ECG to show an appropriate cardiac response.*
- *Only small doses of ß blockers should be used in treating divers.*
- *No matter what drug is used, a trial period of 3-4 weeks prior to diving should be observed to rule out adverse side effects and drug idiosyncrasy.*

ANTIHISTAMINES
eg. Pheniramine, Promethazine, Chlorpheniramine Terfenadine Astemizole Loratidine

Anti-allergy drugs also used for seasickness prophylaxis.

points to consider

- Commonly cause drowsiness which seems to be enhanced underwater.
- Newer histamine H1 antagonists, eg. terfenadine, astemizole and loratadine do not normally cause drowsiness (but do not have an antiemetic effect either) and would seem to be safest for allergic conditions.
- Terfenadine and astemizole can cause serious cardiac dysrhythmias when combined with ketoconazole or a macrolide antibiotic, eg. erythromycin and roxithromycin.
- *If taken against seasickness, use a sedating preparation, eg. promethazine the evening before diving.*
- *If taken for acute allergic rhinitis, diving is not recommended until all symptoms have settled and Eustachian tube function is normal. A non-sedating preparation is best.*
- *If taken for chronic allergic rhinitis, use a non-sedating preparation and ensure Eustachian tube function is normal.*

ANTI-MALARIAL DRUGS

points to consider

- Commonly taken by divers visiting tropical areas (where diving in warm water is popular).
- Mefloquine (Lariam) can commonly cause dizziness, disturbances of balance and nausea. It can also cause bradycardia (especially if taken with ß blockers), visual disturbances, spatial disorientation, muscle aches and pains.

■ *Divers should avoid mefloquine, preferring chloroquine, pyrimethamine/dapsone (Maloprim) and doxycycline.*

BRONCHODILATORS
eg. Aminophylline
Salbutamol

points to consider very seriously

- The presence of bronchoconstriction requiring bronchodilation is a contraindication to diving due to the increased risk of pulmonary barotrauma.
- Bronchodilator aerosols may have an incomplete effect, leaving residual pockets of air trapping in the lung.
- Aminophylline has been shown to not only relax the bronchial smooth muscle but also the pulmonary arteriolar smooth muscle, reducing the efficacy of the pulmonary vascular filter and predisposing to arterial gas embolism.
- Both theophylline and ß selective adrenergic drugs can cause cardiac dysrhythmias.

■ *Diving is contraindicated.*

CAFFEINE
Coffee
Cola

point to consider

- High consumption increases blood pressure and can induce cardiac dysrhythmias.

COCAINE
"Crack"

points to consider very seriously

About 1-2% of 20-30 year olds use the drug in Australia.

- The mood is altered dramatically, with feelings of euphoria reducing the perception of danger.
- It causes restlessness, tremors, loss of coordination and reduced sense of fatigue.
- Intense vasoconstriction causes increases in blood pressure and pulse rate.
- Causes sudden cardiac death syndrome in athletes.
- Withdrawal can cause severe depression.
- Recurrent snorting causes nasal mucosal congestion, predisposing to sinus and aural barotrauma.

■ *Diving is contraindicated.*

CYTOTOXIC DRUGS

eg. Cyclophosphamide, Chlorambucil, Methotrexate

points to consider very seriously

- The reasons for taking such drugs must be carefully assessed, eg. malignant or rheumatic conditions.
- Nausea and vomiting are very common and persistent side effects.
- Many cytotoxics commonly cause pulmonary toxicity, the commonest form being pneumonitis/fibrosis.
- Most patients have some residual functional impairment despite withdrawal of the drug.

Bleomycin

points to consider very seriously

- A cytotoxic drug worthy of individual mention.
- Used in the treatment of testicular teratoma.
- Causes pulmonary toxicity in 4% of patients, usually in the form of pneumonitis/fibrosis.
- The mortality of the pulmonary fibrosis approaches 50%.
- Even in patients with no obvious pulmonary toxicity, the lungs are sensitised to raised levels of inspired oxygen, causing an adult respiratory distress syndrome.
- Anyone who has had bleomycin should not be exposed to partial pressures of oxygen greater than 0.3 ATA.

- *Diving is contraindicated, even after the bleomycin has been discontinued.*

A 22 year old male had a history fo a teratoma of his right testicle for which an orchidectomy had been performed and a course of bleomycin had been completed. In view of the bleomycin causing sensitisation of the lungs to pulmonary toxicity he was classed unfit to dive.

DECONGESTANTS

eg. Pseudoephedrine

points to consider

- Probably the most common drugs used during diving.
- Frequently (and inadvisably) used to aid middle ear equalisation, especially if there is upper respiratory congestion.
- Many decongestants also contain an antihistamine.
- Pseudoephedrine used prophylactically may reduce the incidence of aural barotrauma.
- Pseudoephedrine can cause tachycardia, palpitations, anxiety, vertigo, drowsiness and, rarely, hallucinations.
- Use of pseudoephedrine whilst diving seems to be associated with an increased incidence of aural and sinus barotrauma of ascent.
- Sympathomimetic stimulation may enhance nitrogen narcosis and reduce the convulsive threshold for oxygen toxicity (especially relevant if breathing enriched air).

- *Although very widely used, safety of use before diving is not established and is not recommended.*
- *Diving is not recommended if there is any upper respiratory congestion, especially if Eustachian tube function is compromised.*
- *Whatever is recommended, divers will always use decongestants before and during a diving holiday to aid Eustachian tube function if upper respiratory congestion or mild aural barotrauma threatens to interfere with their diving.*
- *Should they be used against advice, the diver should check against idiosyncratic reactions by taking on a non-diving day.*
- *They must never be used before deep diving or when using enriched air.*

DIURETICS

eg. Frusemide, Chlorthalidone, Hydrochlorothiazide, Amiloride

points to consider

- Assess the reason for its use.
- Prolonged therapy can cause dehydration and electrolyte imbalance (which can be aggravated by seasickness).
- Other side effects include weakness, fatigue, lightheadedness and dizziness.

On a weekend diving trip with 20 medical personnel as divers, 5 were noted to be taking pseudoephedrine as prophylaxis for minor upper respiratory symptoms.

H$_2$ RECEPTOR BLOCKERS
eg. Cimetidine, Ranitidine, Famotidine

points to consider

- Review reason for taking (eg. reflux, ulceration, side effects of non-steroidal anti-inflammatory drugs).
- Can cause headaches, tiredness, drowsiness but generally well tolerated.

HYPNOTICS
Sleeping tablets

points to consider seriously

- Many hypnotic drugs have a residual effect well into the next day.
- The short-acting bendodiazepines (eg. temazepam and triazolam) have an elimination half life of 5-8 hours and are allowed to be used by air crew.
- Anyone who takes sleeping tablets continually may have an underlying emotional or psychiatric problem.

- *Only short-acting bendodiazepines should be used the night before a recreational dive.*

HYPOGLYCAEMICS

Sulphonylureas
eg. Chlorpropamide Glibenclamide Gliclazide Glipizide

points to consider seriously

- They potentiate glucose stimulated insulin release from ß cells of pancreatic islets.
- Their most important side effect is hypoglycaemia.
- They interact with several drugs to lower blood glucose, especially with aspirin, non-steroidal anti-inflammatory and sulphonamide drugs (but also allopurinol, ACE inhibitors, ß blockers, clofibrate and warfarin).

Biguanides
eg. Metformin

- Increases glucose uptake of skeletal muscle and fat.
- Since they do not stimulate insulin release, they do not cause hypoglycaemia as easily.

- *Diving is not recommended.*

INSULIN

points to consider very seriously

- Can cause hypoglycaemia with sudden loss of consciousness.
- Insulin requirements will increase with heavy exercise.
- The more stable and long standing the diabetic, the fewer warning signs of hypoglycaemia will occur.
- Underwater, the symptoms of hypoglycaemia may be modified (eg. no sweating).

- *It is strongly recommended not to dive.*

LIPID LOWERING DRUGS
**eg. Simvastin
Gemfibrozil**

points to consider

- Taken by persons with a high serum cholesterol not controlled by diet alone.
- High cholesterol is a risk factor for coronary heart disease.
- Side effects include a myopathy with malaise, myalgia and fatigue.
- Side effects of paraesthesia and neuropathy have recently been reported.
- *Any diver on lipid lowering drugs should have a careful history taken for coronary artery disease and an ECG should be performed.*

MARIJUANA
**Cannabis
Delta 9
  tetrahydrocannabinol**

points to consider very seriously

- The commonest "recreational" drug.
- Thirty per cent of 20-25 year olds are estimated to use it in Australia.
- It impairs memory, coordination and balance.
- The associated feelings of euphoria will reduce the perception of danger.
- Causes mild sedation and increases the heart rate.
- Vasodilation can reduce the blood pressure and increase heat loss.
- One "joint" will affect the smoker for at least eight hours.
- *Diving is contraindicated.*

NON-STEROID ANTI INFLAMMATORY DRUGS NSAIDS
**eg. Indomethacin
Diclofenac
Naproxen**

points to consider

- Consider the reason for taking.
- The commonest side effects are heartburn, nausea and abdominal pain. Headache, dizziness, drowsiness and tinnitus can also occur.
- Asthma can be exacerbated even years since the last attack.
- Must be taken with food or antacid (difficult if seasick).

OPIATES

**eg. Heroin
Morphia
Pethidine**

points to consider very seriously

- Produce alterations in mood and reduce coordination and reaction time.
- Causes sedation.

▪ *Diving is contraindicated.*

ORAL CONTRACEPTIVES

"The pill"

points to consider

- It has been hypothesised to increase the risks of decompression sickness by increasing the coagulability of the blood.
- There is no evidence that this occurs.

▪ *Diving would seem to be safe.*

STEROIDS

**eg. Prednisone
Prednisolone**

points to consider seriously

- Potent anti-inflammatory drugs.
- Beware of the underlying condition necessitating their use.
- Enhances oxygen toxicity (especially relevant if using enriched air).
- Prolonged steroid intake with relatively large doses will cause a Cushing's Syndrome, including disturbed carbohydrate tolerance, osteoporosis, electrolyte disturbances, hypertension, proximal myopathy and even mental disturbances.

▪ *A full assessment of the underlying condition and possible side effects of the steroids must be made before diving is recommended.*

STEROID INHALERS

**eg. Beclomethasone
Budesonide
Salmeterol**

points to seriously consider

- Inhaled in the treatment of asthma.
- Used intranasally in the treatment of allergic rhinitis.
- Epistaxis and haemorrhagic nasal secretions may occur with intranasal use.

▪ *If used in the treatment of asthma, diving is contraindicated.*
▪ *If used for allergic rhinitis, diving may be considered if there are no acute symptoms and Eustachian tube function is normal.*

TOBACCO
Nicotine

points to consider seriously

- Causes vasoconstriction, increasing blood pressure and heart rate.
- Coronary artery vasoconstriction can occur.
  (See under "smoking" for other interesting facts).

TRANQUILLISERS
**eg. Diazepam
Oxazepam
Chlordiazepoxide
Alprazolam**

points to consider very seriously

- Consider the reason for taking the tranquilliser.
- Common side effects are fatigue, drowsiness, muscle weakness and ataxia.
- Nitrogen narcosis will be enhanced.
- Many tranquillisers (eg. diazepam) have long half lives (80 hrs).

- *It is strongly recommended not to dive.*

A 23 year old Swedish male had been taking Diazepam 5mg twice daily for two years for an anxiety condition. He was now travelling the world and felt that he had left his anxieties, mainly related to his working conditions, behind him. He now wished to experience the "relaxation" of diving. In view of the chronicity of his anxiety condition and the sedative side effects of his medication he was classed unfit to dive. He was advised to slowly reduce the dosage of his medication over the following month and confirm the resolution of his symptoms without medication. He could then be reassessed.

A 22 year old Australian female was taking oxazepam 30mg three times a day for chronic anxiety. She said that she "did not really need them now" and they had "no side effects". She was classed unfit to dive and asked to see her general practitioner for review of her medication.

A 28 year old female diver began suffering severe headaches on the second day of a week's diving holiday on the Great Barrier Reef. She was evacuated to the mainland after two days.

When her BP was measured it was found to be 190/120. Further questioning discovered that she was taking phentermine (Duromine), an appetite suppressant to reduce her weight before going home. Moreover, after her first dive she had been given pseudoephedrine 60mg three times daily by a fellow diver for a stuffy nose and difficulty equalising her ears. The drug interaction had caused a precipitate rise in her BP which duly returned to normal with cessation of both drugs.

Ear, Nose and Throat

- The middle ear is the only air-containing organ which needs active pressure equalisation whilst diving.
- The middle ear is the organ most commonly injured whilst diving.
- The tympanic membrane is about ten times bigger than the oval window. The ossicles give a leverage advantage of 1.7 to 1.
- These mechanisms may lead to round or oval window rupture or damage to the membranes within the inner ear during equalisation.
- The sinuses equalise pressure with the paranasal spaces passively.
- Vertigo and vomiting, common symptoms of inner ear pathology, are extremely dangerous if experienced underwater.
- Hearing is not an essential sense whilst diving recreationally underwater.
- There are numerous methods of equalising the middle ear. (See Appendix A).

UPPER RESPIRATORY TRACT

ALLERGIC RHINITIS   points to consider

- Causes nasal mucosal swelling and rhinorrhea.
- Predisposes to both sinus and aural barotrauma.
- Sneezing through a regulator underwater tends to dislodge the regulator.
- Commonly occurs in atopic people who also have asthma.
- Commonly controlled with antihistamine drugs.

- *Whilst suffering the symptoms of allergic rhinitis, it is strongly recommended not to dive.*
- *Antihistamines used to control allergic rhinitis should be non-sedating.*

BIFID UVULA   points to consider

- Occurs in 2-3% of children.
- It is considered a partial cleft palate of the smallest degree.
- Can be associated with hypoplasia of the Eustachian tube.
- *It is essential to confirm normal Eustachian tube function.*

A 26 year old Norwegian had come to Australia to "dive the Barrier Reef". On arrival in Australia he developed an allergic rhinitis with constant sneezing and runny nose. He commenced loratidine with only partial control of his symptoms. On his first dive he suffered ear pain on descent but tried to "force it". He ruptured his right drum and was unable to dive for the rest of his diving holiday.

CLEFT PALATE
repaired

points to consider
- Can be associated with hypoplasia of the Eustachian tube.
- Even if good palatal repair is achieved, Eustachian tube dysfunction can persist.
- The teeth can be crowded and deformed, interfering with easy retention of the regulator mouthpiece.

■ *Ensure normal Eustachian tube function and ability to hold a regulator firmly in the mouth.*

LARYNGECTOMY
partial or full

points to consider very seriously
- Reason for the surgery is usually a malignancy.
- The sensation and protective mechanism to the airway are lost, predisposing to aspiration into the trachea.

■ *Diving is contraindicated.*

LARYNGOCELE

An air-filled dilation of the larynx near the vocal cords. Seen in musicians playing large brass instruments!

points to consider seriously
- The swelling enlarges with a Valsalva manoeuvre.
- The swelling may dilate on ascent, possibly causing an obstruction.

■ *Diving is not recommended until after surgical correction.*

NASAL POLYPS

points to consider seriously
- Usually associated with chronic infection, nasal obstruction or allergic rhinitis.
- Predisposes to sinus and aural barotrauma.

■ *Normal Eustachian tube function must be confirmed before diving is recommended.*

■ *Treatment should be advised to avoid possible future complications.*

A 30 year old Australian male who had logged 300 dives began suffering sinus squeeze. Examination and X-ray confirmed nasal polyps. He was treated by a naturopath with nasal drops and when reviewed three months later the nasal polyps had gone. He recommenced diving with no further troubles.

NASAL SEPTAL DEVIATION

The nasal septum is bent or buckled.

points to consider

- Seen commonly, often in divers with no history of nasal trauma.
- In severe cases the deviation interferes with nasal breathing (which is not important whilst diving but will also predispose to sinus and aural barotrauma).
- *Normal Eustachian tube function must be confirmed before diving is recommended.*
- *The diver should be warned of the possibility of sinus barotrauma.*

SINUSITIS

points to consider seriously

- The sinuses normally equalise passively on both descent and ascent, dependent on a patent ostium with the nasal passages.
- History of recurrent sinus congestion or infection with nasal discharge may reflect allergic rhinitis, nasal irritation from tobacco smoke, snorting cocaine, overuse of decongestant drops or mechanical obstruction from nasal polyps or deviated nasal septum.
- All predispose to sinus barotrauma (2/3 occur on descent and 1/3 on ascent).
- Sinus barotrauma is rarely dangerous, usually causing severe facial pain, headache or blood in the mask which may prevent further descent or just make the rest of the day miserable.
- Serious complications can occasionally occur, including pneumocephalus, facial subcutaneous emphysema, orbital haematoma or sinusitis with its complications (eg. brain abscess).
- Many of the causes of sinus barotrauma will also affect Eustachian tube function and predispose to aural barotrauma.
- *Any diver with acute sinusitis is strongly recommended not to dive until full resolution has occurred.*
- *Any diver with a history of recurrent sinus problems should have an ENT specialist assessment.*

A 25 year old British male had a history of recurrent ear infections as a child and had had an operation to "patch" a chronic perforation of the right ear. Examination showed heavy scarring and retraction of the left ear drum. He was failed due to the high risk of aural barotrauma.

TRACHEOSTOMY

point to consider very seriously

- Bypassing the larynx will leave the airway with no protective reflexes or sphincter.

■ *Diving is contraindicated.*

UPPER RESPIRATORY INFECTION
eg. Tonsillitis
Pharyngitis
Laryngitis

points to consider seriously

- The mucosal swelling and increased mucus production of the nasopharynx predisposes to sinus and aural barotrauma.
- Often there is an associated lower respiratory infection.

■ *It is strongly recommended not to dive until full resolution has occurred.*

EXTERNAL EAR

EAR PLUGS

points to consider

- Ear plugs will create an air space in the outer ear between the plug and the tympanic membrane that will lead to a reverse middle ear aural barotrauma of descent. (Also known as "reverse ear" or external ear squeeze)
- This can also be caused by a tight-fitting hood.

■ *Ear plugs must not be worn whilst diving.*

EAR RINGS, NOSE STUDS

points to consider

- Dangling ear rings can become entangled with the mask strap or hood and cause severe lacerations to the pinna.
- Nose studs can be pulled by the edge of the mask, traumatising the nose.
- Tight hoods can push ear studs into the skin over the mastoid area.
- Fish can be attracted by bright ear rings and pull on them quite forcibly with their mouths.

■ *It is advisable to remove all jewellery before diving.*

A 24 year old male went on a "resort dive". Unbeknown to his instructor he wore silicone ear plugs because "he didn't want to get his ears wet". At 3m (10ft) he suffered severe ear pain which he could not ignore and he surfaced. Examination revealed a grade IV left aural barotrauma. The diver was very annoyed and threatened to sue the diving instructor for his holiday expenses because he hadn't been told not to wear ear plugs.

EAR WAX

points to consider

- Ear wax is formed in the outer third of the external canal.
- It is produced continuously and provides waterproofing of the skin of the outer ear.
- If it is pushed inwards by washing, swimming, finger or cotton bud it will tend to accumulate and form plugs.
- If impacted, ear wax can form an ear plug with similar consequences.
- Excessive ear wax will cause water retention in the outer ear, predisposing to otitis externa.

- *Any large plugs of wax that occlude the external ear canal should be removed to enable the tympanic membrane to be adequately examined, and to prevent reverse middle ear barotrauma of descent and otitis externa.*

EXOSTOSES

Bony growths on the walls of the external ear canal which narrow the canal.

points to consider

- The narrowed canal is more prone to blockage by wax or debris, and more susceptible to otitis externa.
- An exostosis on the floor of the external canal can form a sump which retains moisture and predisposes to infection.

- *Advice on prophylactic measures should be given in writing. (See Appendix B).*
- *Advise that ears should be visually checked before any diving expeditions.*

OTITIS EXTERNA
Swimmer's ear
Diver's ear
Coral ear
Surfer's ear

An infection of the skin of the external canal.

points to consider

- The infection is not a danger to the diver but can be extremely painful.
- The infection will be aggravated by prolonged immersion.
- If recurrent or chronic, the infection becomes very difficult to eradicate.

- *Once treated, advice must be given to help prevent recurrence (See Appendix B).*
- *Any diver visiting tropical waters should be advised on prophylactic measures (see Appendix B).*

TYMPANIC MEMBRANE AND MIDDLE EAR

CHOLESTEATOMA   Presence of squamous epithelial sac within the middle ear cleft.

points to consider very seriously

- There is a disruption of the architecture of the middle ear and surrounding tissues.
- Causes a chronic discharge and often a peripheral perforation of the tympanic membrane.
- Erosion of bone and the ossicles and formation of granulation tissue and polyps may occur.
- A difficult condition to treat and often becomes chronic. Treatment may require surgical removal of diseased bone and cholesteatoma, creating a smooth wide cavity lined by skin.
- Deafness is inevitable.

- *It is strongly recommended not to dive, even after treatment.*

EFFUSION
serous

Fluid in the middle ear.

points to consider seriously

- Usually reflects poor Eustachian tube function.
- Consider the underlying pathology (eg. nasopharyngeal infections, allergies, obstructions and tumours; and recent aural barotrauma from flying or diving).
- Normal equalisation of the middle ear will be compromised.

- *It is strongly recommended not to dive until the effusion has been absorbed or drained and normal Eustachian tube function confirmed.*

A 22 year old male was noted to have bilateral middle ear effusions during his routine diving medical. He gave no history of hearing problems but a subsequent audiogram revealed a moderate bilateral conductive deafness. Although he could demonstrate a normal Eustachian tube function he was declared unfit to dive pending an ENT opinion and full resolution of his effusions.

A 21 year old female diver developed severe pain in both ears whilst on a week's holiday on a diving boat 320km (200 miles) offshore in the Coral Sea. The pain became so severe she was evacuated by sea plane to the mainland. Examination confirmed otitis externa with a small boil in the right ear. She was admitted to hospital for incision of the boil, strong analgesia and antibiotic therapy.

GROMMETS
Tube myringotomy

Small aerating tubes placed through the tympanic membrane.

points to consider seriously

- Usually inserted because of inadequate Eustachian tube function.
- They will allow water to enter the middle ear, possibly causing vertigo and/or infection.
- They are usually extruded spontaneously, sometimes before the reason for their insertion has resolved.
- They may cause tympanosclerosis, which is not usually symptomatic.
- *Diving is contraindicated whilst grommets are in situ.*
- *After extrusion, the middle ear and Eustachian tube function must be confirmed to be normal before diving may be considered.*

MASTOIDECTOMY
simple

Removal of the cortex of the mastoid and opening of all the cells and antrum.

points to consider

- Consider the underlying pathology.
- Performed usually for acute mastoiditis not settling with antibiotics alone.
- The mastoid antrum is drained but the middle ear and external meatus remain intact.
- *If there is no chronic pathology, the operative site is fully healed and Eustachain tube function is normal, diving may be considered.*

RADICAL MASTOIDECTOMY
modified

Excision of the mastoid cells or mastoid process of the temporal bone (often in association with tympanoplasty).

points to consider very seriously

- Performed when infection or cholesteatoma extend into the mastoid process.
- Usually accompanied by significant hearing loss.
- The external ear often becomes combined with the mastoid space to form a large cavity, allowing cold water to produce a significant calorific effect on the labyrinth, causing vertigo.
- Some newer surgical techniques maintain the integrity of the middle ear.
- *It is strongly recommended not to dive if the mastoid space is combined with the external ear.*

| **MONOMERIC TYMPANIC MEMBRANE** | Part of a tympanic membrane which has healed by forming only one of its three layers. |

Seen as a "blow out" from the tympanic membrane during equalisation.

points to consider

- Reflects previous ear pathology which may not have resolved.
- Because of its distensibility, it may be more liable to perforation.

  ▪ *Divers should be warned of the possible complications.*

MYRINGOPLASTY

Surgical restoration of a perforated tympanic membrane by grafting.

point to consider

- Consider the cause for the perforation and the reason it did not heal spontaneously.

  ▪ *If: (i) the grafted membrane shows normal movement with equalisation of the middle ear and (ii) the graft is stable and not prone to infection, diving may be considered.*

PERFORATION OF TYMPANIC MEMBRANE
Ruptured ear drum

points to consider very seriously

- Consider any underlying middle ear pathology to cause the perforation.
- Diving with a perforation will allow water into the middle ear with possible vertigo or infection.
- Suppurative otitis media can become chronic with secondary hearing loss.
- Several experienced divers who have huge perforations of their tympanic membranes dive quite safely (with their hearing loss).

  ▪ *It is strongly recommended not to dive with any perforation of the tympanic membrane.*

  ▪ *Acute perforations should be given adequate time to heal – at least six weeks.*

  ▪ *Chronic perforations should be surgically repaired before diving.*

A 54 year old Australain male had been diving for 25 years. When seen for another complaint a large perforation of his tympanic membrane was noted. There was very little of the tympanic membrane left! His hearing in that ear was predictably very poor. He refused all treatment and against all advice he continued to dive. It was interesting that he used an ear plug to keep the water out of the middle ear and equalised the middle ear cavity in the normal fashion.

STAPEDECTOMY

Excision of the stapes in the middle ear and replacement by a prosthesis.

points to consider very seriously

- Excessive middle ear equalisation will subject the oval window to excessive movement with danger of rupture and damage to the middle ear.
- Modern surgical techniques (such as Jean-Bernard Causse technique) are claimed to make diving after stapedectomy reasonably safe.

- *It is strongly recommended not to dive.*
- *If newer surgical techniques have been used, an ENT opinion should be obtained before diving is considered.*

TYMPANOPLASTY
Middle ear surgery

Surgical restoration of the hearing mechanism of the middle ear with restoration of the drum membrane to protect the round window and establishment of ossicular continuity.

point to consider seriously

- Having once been reconstructed, barotrauma to the middle ear could be more serious and cause permanent damage.

- *Diving is not recommended.*

INNER EAR

LABRYNTHITIS

points to consider seriously

- Symptoms include nausea, vomiting and vertigo.
- If chronic, it is often associated with cholesteatoma or middle ear infection.

- *Diving is not recommended until complete resolution of all symptoms and return to normal ear function.*
- *If recurring or chronic, it is strongly recommended not to dive.*

MENIERE'S DISEASE
Labryinthus hydrops

Dilation of the endolymphatic system of the inner ear with denervation of the sensory elements of the cochlea and vestibular apparatus.

points to consider seriously

- Symptoms include sudden attacks of vertigo, nausea and vomiting.
- Causes a progressive hearing loss.
- Even after surgery (such as labyrinthectomy, endolymphatic shunts, vestibular nerve section), inner ear dysfunction remains with greater risks of inner ear barotrauma.

- *It is strongly recommended not to dive.*

POSITIONAL VERTIGO
Spontaneous
Post-traumatic

points to consider

- Considered to be a degenerative condition of the utricular and saccular maculae.
- Often seen in patients with a history of a head injury.

- *It is strongly recommended not to dive until full resolution and no attacks have occurred for at least six months.*

DEAFNESS

points to consider

- Deafness is usually associated with pathology of the outer, middle or inner ear.
- A congenitally deaf ear may be malformed, impeding equalisation of a middle ear cavity.
- Hearing is not an important sense underwater, except for detecting approaching boat engines and ascent rate alarms on dive computers (which could be replaced/enhanced by a flashing signal).
- Middle ear barotrauma is the commonest injury that occurs whilst diving. It could result in hearing loss.
- It would be a tragedy for a partially deaf diver to unnecessarily lose more of their hearing.
- A totally deaf diver can lose no more hearing.
- Deaf divers using sign language underwater are able to communicate much more effectively than normal hearing divers.
- The Mary Hair Grammar School for the Deaf in Newbury, England, which is the only "high" school especially for the deaf in the United Kingdom, has its own scuba club.

- *A totally deaf diver should be allowed to dive provided that the ear's architecture allows normal equalisation and the underlying pathology itself does not preclude diving.*
- *Confirm the ear's architecture if necessary by CAT scan.*
- *Partially deaf divers are not recommended to dive.*

  If highly motivated, the underlying pathology must not preclude diving and ear architecture must allow normal equalisation.

  The full risks of aural barotrauma and the danger of further hearing loss and its implications must be fully explained.
- *An audiogram must first be performed.*

Endocrine

- Endocrine diseases commonly have insidious onset and affect many systems.
- All such diseases need to be fully investigated and fully treated before diving can be considered.
- Consider the presence of underlying disease causing the endocrine abnormality (eg. tuberculosis or sarcoid destruction of the adrenal).
- Consider all possible complications (eg. diabetes in Cushing's Syndrome).
- The commonest endocrine diseases are diabetes and thyroid disease.

DIABETES MELLITUS

points to consider very seriously

- Hypoglycaemia attacks are a well recognised complication of diabetic treatment.
- Hypoglycaemia can cause confusion, sweating, fast heartbeat, altered consciousness and neurological symptoms (eg. hemiplegia).
- Hypoglycaemic attacks can occur with both insulin and oral hypoglycaemic drug treatment.
- Rational thinking can be impaired with hypoglycaemia. A diabetic may deny feeling abnormal and reject attempts to give sugar.
- Warning symptoms of hypoglycaemia may be lost in long-standing, well-controlled diabetes, so that loss of consciousness may occur without warning.
- Symptoms of hypoglycaemia may be more difficult to identify underwater with the distraction of underwater equipment and environment.
- Maturity onset diabetics are often obese and physically unfit.
- Complications of diabetes include premature onset of coronary artery disease, peripheral vascular disease and autonomic neuropathy.
- Exercise will increase the rate of mobilisation of insulin from a subcutaneous site on an exercising limb.
- Blood glucose has been shown to fall significantly during hyperbaric treatment of diabetic patients but to remain static or rise in controls.

A 23 year old Australian male soldier was found to have heavy glycosuria. A 2 hour post prandial blood glucose confirmed diabetes mellitus and he was classed unfit to dive and referred to his medical officer for immediate treatment.

- *Most diving doctors would consider insulin-dependent diabeties a contraindication to dive.*
- *Diabetics on hypoglycaemic drugs are strongly recommended not to dive.*
- *Some doctors (excluding the author) would consider diabetics on hypoglycaemic agents fit to dive if they have:*
  - *had no hypoglycaemic attacks or diabetic complications for at least a year*
  - *no evidence of neuropathy, microvascular disease or microalbuminuria*
  - *no evidence of ischaemic heart disease on stress testing.*
  - *good long term control reflected by a normal HbA_{1c}*
  - *a normal body mass index and perform regular physical exercise*
  - *a good understanding of the nature of their disease and the risks they are taking*
  - *a letter from their endocrinologist confirming the stability of their diabetes*
- *Diabetics controlled purely by diet should have a normal body mass index, no evidence of complications and perform regular physical exercise.*
- *All diabetic divers should have an annual diving medical.*

THYROID DISEASE
**Hyperthyroidism
Grave's Disease
Hypothyroidism
Thyroiditis**

points to consider seriously

- Hyperthyroidism can cause tachycardia and more serious cardiac dysrhythmias, heart failure, muscular weakness, periodic paralysis (in Chinese people).
- Hyperthyroid patients treated with thionamide drugs will relapse in 50% of cases.
- Many hyperthyroid patients treated by surgery or radioactive iodine later become hypothyroid.
- Hypothyroidism can cause general malaise, lethargy, slowing of the reflexes, bradycardia and heart failure.
- Thyroid function alters very slowly with drug treatment.

- *Any diver with thyroid disease should not dive until thyroid function is normal and stable.*
- *Any diver with a history of thyroid disease should have their cardiovascular system critically assessed and have had their thyroid function checked within the previous three months.*

Eyes

- Whilst diving it is necessary to be able to
  - read pressure and depth gauges and/or dive computers
  - clearly see one's buddy
  - see the dive boat from a distance
  - clearly see the underwater terrain (for enjoyment's sake if nothing else).
- Mask squeeze can subject the eyeball and skin of the face to a considerable negative pressure.
- Mask squeeze can be as great a problem whilst free diving as when scuba diving when exhalation from the nose is easier to perform.
- Due to refraction of light at the air/water interface at the mask, the apparent size of objects is increased one third and their distance seems reduced by one quarter.
- The diving mask reduces the peripheral vision and limits the total amount of light.

CATARACTS

points to consider

- After cataract surgery without a lens implant, correction of the visual deficit is essential. Because adequate lenses are so bulky contact lenses will be needed.
- The corneas are slow to heal after surgery.

  - *Diving is not recommended for at least a year after cataract surgery.*
  - *Providing vision is adequate (with gas permeable contact lenses if necessary), diving may then be considered.*

COLOUR BLINDNESS

point to consider

- Normal colour vision is not necessary in recreational diving.

CONTACT LENSES

points to consider

- Widely used underwater.
- Contact lenses may be hard and small (diameter about 9.0mm) which "float" on the cornea, or soft and larger (diameter about 14mm) which adhere closely to the cornea and move less.
- A major concern during diving is lens loss when the mask becomes flooded. This is more likely with the smaller, hard lens, and when near or on the surface due to wave action.
- Soft lenses are all gas permeable, but only cover the range +4 to -9 diopters.
- Some conditions demand hard lenses (eg. astigmatism >2 diopters, kerato-conus, corneal scars and corneal grafts).
- Modern hard lenses are made from a range of materials which have varying gas permeability.
- Divers wearing the older gas impermeable hard lenses (made from PMMA which is very hardwearing and can last 20 years!) have been observed to have bubble formation under their lenses on decompression. This caused nummular patches of corneal epithelial oedema. No permanent damage, however, is normally caused by such bubble formation.

  [To check what sort of hard lens a diver uses, ask how it is stored. A gas impermeable hard lens is usually stored dry whilst a gas permeable hard lens must be stored wet].

- Bubbles formed under a gas impermeable hard lens can be flushed out by frequent blinking as 14-20% of the tear volume between a properly-fitted lens and the cornea should be exchanged with each blink – the so called "lens pump".
- Bubble formation under the gas impermeable hard lens can be avoided by making a 0.4mm fenestration in the centre of the lens.

A 19 year old French female had her mask accidently kicked off by her buddy as they swam through a tunnel in the reef. Her hard contact lenses were both washed out of her eyes. She clawed her way out of the tunnel towards the light sustaining severe abrasions and lacerations to her arms and hands. Her buddy was unaware of her plight so she ascended slowly to the surface where although she could not see the dive boat managed to gain the attention of the lookout with her whistle.

Contact Lenses
(continued)

■ *Any contact lens worn whilst diving should be gas permeable.*

■ *Unless contraindicated, disposable soft contact lenses are best suited for diving.*

■ *Hard contact lenses should be made from materials with high gas permeability.*

■ *When the mask is taken off or flooded, the diver should squint to minimise the danger of losing the lens.*

■ *Hard contact lenses especially must be properly fitted.*

■ *All divers should be advised on possible complications with the use of contact lenses (viz. loss, trauma to the cornea, infection).*

■ *To reduce the likelihood of infection, the lenses should not be worn overnight.*

CORNEAL TRANSPLANTS

points to consider seriously

● The corneal wound encompasses the whole corneal circumference.

● The cornea is very slow to heal.

● The cornea can be exposed to high negative pressures with mask squeeze.

■ *Diving is not recommended for at least a year after a corneal transplant and at least a month after the removal of the stitches.*

GLAUCOMA

points to consider

● Visual acuity must be adequate to dive.

● Treatment may include use of ß blocker eye drops with possible, but unlikely, side effects on the cardiovascular system.

● Some surgical treatments of glaucoma are designed to allow spontaneous drainage of aqueous humour from the anterior chamber into the subconjunctival area. Any negative pressure applied to the eyeball will draw aqueous humour out of the eyeball.

■ *Some of these surgical procedures are a contraindication to both scuba and free diving.*

■ *Systemic absorption of eye drops can be minimised by pressure on the lacrimal puncta for two minutes after instillation of the drop into the lower conjunctival sac.*

■ *Side effects of ß blockers are then most unlikely but should still should be excluded before diving is recommended.*

PRESCRIPTION LENSES IN FACE MASKS

points to consider

- Many dive shops and schools stock ready-made minus spherical form prescription lenses, ready for instant fitting into one or two mask apertures.

- This often ignores any astigmatism present, reducing visual acuity.

- There is also no adjustment of the lense's optical centres to the interpupillary distance. There may be discrepancies of up to 10mm (0.4 in) off-centre causing eye strain and double vision.

- *Professionally prescribed and fitted lenses bonded permanently to the inside surface of the mask are recommended.*

RADIAL KEROTOTOMY

Radial incisions made in the cornea to increase the peripheral curvature of the cornea so that the central area is flattened.

points to consider seriously

- The radial incisions should penetrate the corneal stroma no deeper than the level of Descemet's membrane. The structure of the cornea is weakened by these incisions.

- Leakage of aqueous humour is an occasional complication of the procedure, reflecting possible full thickness penetration of the cornea.

- There have been suggestions that severe mask squeeze could endanger the integrity of the eyeball.

- There are no recorded cases of damage to the cornea following radial keratotomy due to mask squeeze.

- There is diverse opinion as to the full healing time for the radial incisions.

- Many divers have had radial keratotomy in order to dive without the hindrance of contact lenses.

- *It is recommended not to dive for a year following radial keratotomy.*

- *Diving may then be considered, but the diver should be warned of the theoretical danger of severe mask squeeze and advised to avoid it by exhaling frequently through the nose.*

- *Newer techniques for corneal refractive surgery (eg. excimer laser keratotomy and laminar keratoplasty) do not involve deep penetration of the cornea and should therefore be used by divers in the future.*

RETINAL DETACHMENT

points to consider

- Consider the underlying pathology for the detachment.
- Some surgical treatments may deliberately leave a small amount of gas in the eyeball which can remain for lenghty periods.

■ *Any diver having surgery for retinal detachment must confirm with the surgeon whether there is any gas in the eyeball, the nature of the gas and the time of its elimination. Both diving and flying is normally prohibited for this time.*

■ *If fully repaired, diving may be considered (but no bungy jumping!).*

VISUAL ACUITY

points to consider

- The diver must be able to see their gauges and the surrounds clearly.
- Australian standards for commercial divers require an uncorrected visual acuity of 6/36m (20/120ft) Snellen in each eye, and 6/24m (20/80ft) with both eyes for distance; N24 in each eye and N18 with both eyes for near vision.
- North Sea standards require an uncorrected visual acuity of 6/24m (20/80ft) in each eye.

■ *Corrective lenses are recommended for any diver with a visual acuity of 6/24m (20/80ft) or less, or near vision N24 or less.*

Gastrointestinal

- Any condition which can cause air trapping in any of the intestine can cause rupture of that intestine on ascent.
- There are 12 cases of gastric rupture whilst scuba diving in the literature.
- Head-down positions are common whilst diving.
- Vomiting underwater is very dangerous (even if practiced!).
- Chronic inflammation of the intestine can be associated with malabsorption and general debility.

OESOPHAGEAL CONDITIONS

ACHALASIA

Ineffective and later absent peristalsis in the body of the oesophagus with loss of coordinated relaxation of the lower oesophageal sphincter.

points to consider seriously

- Atony and dilation of the lower oesophagus occur.
- There is a danger of pooling of food and secretions in the lower oesophagus.
- *Diving is not recommended.*

Oesophageal DIVERTICULA

point to consider seriously

- Secretions can accumulate in the diverticula and aspirate when in the head down position during diving.
- *Diving is not recommended until after surgical correction.*

GASTRO-OESOPHAGEAL REFLUX

point to consider seriously

- Free gastro-oesophageal reflux may lead to regurgitation and possible aspiration of gastric contents into the lungs or regulator when in a head-down position.
- *Diving is not recommended.*

HIATUS HERNIA

points to consider seriously

- A non-symptomatic sliding hiatus hernia should give no problem whilst diving.
- An incarcerated sliding or paraoesophageal hiatus hernia risks overdistension and possible gastric rupture of the gastric remnant in the hernia.
- Patients who have had surgical repair of their hiatus hernia (eg. fundoplication) can suffer from "gas bloat" syndrome, with gaseous distension of the stomach.

- *An incarcerated or paraoesophageal hiatus hernia is a contraindication to diving, even after repair.*

diffuse OESOPHAGEAL SPASM

A syndrome of painful dysphagia marked by regurgitation and choking.

point to consider

- The pain is often precipitated by cold liquids.

- *Diving is not recommended.*

SCLERODERMA OF THE OESOPHAGUS

points to consider very seriously

- Increased collagen and fibrosis in the lower 2/3 of the oesophagus cause hypomotility.
- Loss of function in the lower oesophageal sphincter results in gastrooesophageal reflux.
- Involvement of other systems (eg. the lung) will disqualify from diving anyway.

- *It is strongly recommended not to dive.*

GASTRIC CONDITIONS

GASTRIC OUTLET OBSTRUCTION
Pyloric stenosis

points to consider seriously

- Frequent vomiting is a common symptom.
- Gastric distension is frequent.
- Often causes malnutrition and anaemia.

- *Diving is not recommended.*

**PARTIAL
AFFERENT LOOP
OBSTRUCTION**

points to consider seriously

- Occurs in patients with a sub-total gastrectomy with a gastrojejeunostomy.
- Dilation of the afferent loop with pancreatic and biliary secretions can occur.
- Sometimes caused by stenosis in the afferent loop.

- *Diving is not recommended.*

**PEPTIC
ULCERATION**

points to consider seriously

- Symptoms can be sudden, severe and disabling.
- Insidious bleeding can cause iron deficiency anaemia.

- *If symptomatic, it is strongly recommended not to dive.*
- *If symptom free for over a month, even on treatment, diving may be considered.*

**POSTGASTRECTOMY
SYNDROMES**
**Dumping syndrome
Afferent loop syndrome
Small stomach syndrome**

Associated with rapid gastric emptying.

point to consider seriously.

- In severe cases it can be associated with vomiting, faintness, palpitations, flushing, and lassitude after meals.

- *Diving is not recommended.*

**Late Dumping
Syndrome**

Attributed to a reactive hypoglycaemia

point to consider seriously

- Causes diaphoresis, palpitations, lassitude, mental confusion and even loss of consciousness 30-180 minutes after a meal.

- *Diving is not recommended.*

**RECURRENT
VOMITING**
**eg. Cyclical vomiting
Abdominal migraine
Psychogenic vomiting**

points to consider seriously

- Occurs in young adults.
- Can cause metabolic derangement.
- Beware of undiagnosed pathology.

- *Diving is not recommended.*

CONDITIONS OF SMALL AND LARGE INTESTINES AND ASSOCIATED ORGANS

COLOSTOMY
ILEOSTOMY

points to consider seriously

- A "continent" ileostomy (eg. Koch Pouch) can trap air with possible rupture on ascent.
- The normal colostomy and ileostomy stomas do not cause problems.

DIVERTICULAR DISEASE of the large intestine

- Is not a problem.

GALLSTONES
Biliary colic

points to consider seriously

- Biliary colic causes sudden incapacitation with severe pain, nausea and vomiting.
- Symptomless gallstones should not affect diving.

- *Diving is not recommended if there has been a recent history of biliary colic.*

INFLAMMATORY BOWEL DISEASE
Crohn's Disease
Ulcerative Colitis
Regional Colitis

points to seriously consider

- Often a chronic problem with generalised ill health and continuous or intermittent diarrhoea.
- Commonly presents in the 20 to 40-year-old group.
- May be intermittent with long periods of remission.
- Complications include anaemia, electrolyte imbalance producing lethargy, malabsorption, liver disease and renal stones.
- Commonly treated with sulphasalazine and steroids.
- Sulphasalazine can cause nausea, vomiting and anorexia but these are minimised using the enteric-coated preparation. Rare side effects include haematological disorders and fibrosing alveolitis.
- Iatrogenic steroid disease can be a complication of prolonged high dose steroid intake. (See under "steroids" on Page 56)

- *Diving is not recommended during an acute exacerbation.*
- *Diving during remissions may be considered in the absence of any long term complications (eg. anaemia), the absence of any disabling drug side effect and if general physical fitness has been maintained.*
- *Divers on long term steroids should be screened for iatrogenic steroid disease.*

recurring
SMALL BOWEL OBSTRUCTION
Pseudoobstruction

points to consider seriously

- Consider any underlying pathology.
- Often associated with distension of the small bowel.
- Whether chronic or recurring, overdistension of the small bowel could occur on ascent.
- Rupture of the small bowel is most unlikely.

chronic or recurring
PANCREATITIS

points to consider seriously

- Many such patients are debilitated.
- Sometimes associated with alcohol abuse.
- Can lead to diabetes and malabsorption.

- *Diving is not recommended.*

A 26 year old Italian male had a four year history of ulcerative colitis. He was taking sulphasalazine and 5mg prednisolone daily. He had 1-2 semi-fluid bowels actions daily and occasional pains. He had been travelling continually for the previous six months with no problems and jogged daily. His examination was unremarkable and his blood sugar normal and he was classed fit to dive.

Gynaecology

PREGNANCY

points to consider very seriously

The certainties:

- Nausea and vomiting commonly occur, especially during the first trimester.
- An expanding waistline, especially in the third trimester can cause problems fitting the wet suit and weight belt and can interfere with mobility, especially exiting the water and boarding small boats.
- Enlargement of the breasts can cause discomfort when wearing wet suits.
- The growing uterus interferes with respiratory function, especially in the third trimester, limiting exercise tolerance.

The uncertainties:

- Increased fluid retention during the second trimester onwards could interfere with Eustachian tube function.
- Increased fluid retention could predispose maternal decompression sickness.
- High partial pressures of oxygen, nitrogen and carbon dioxide could have toxic or teratogenic effects on the foetus.
- The foetus could have an increased susceptibility to decompression sickness.
- Venous bubbles bypassing the foetal pulmonary circulation through the foramen ovale could cause cerebral arterial gas embolism.
- Could foetal bubbles have a teratogenic effect?
- *The general recommendation of all diving organisations is not to dive during pregnancy or when trying to become pregnant.*

A 25 year old American female on a six month world tour was one week late for her menstrual period. She and her partner had been using condoms for contraception. A pregnancy test was positive and she was classed unfit to dive until after her pregnancy.

RECENT GYNAECOLOGICAL SURGERY
eg. D&C
Suction termination of pregnancy

points to consider

- There does not seem to be any problem of endometritis in female divers with a patulous cervical os.

- Where the cervical os has been forcibly dilated and the lining of the uterus disrupted there could be a danger of infection.

- *Diving is not recommended for at least two weeks.*

MAMMARY IMPLANTS
Breast implants

points to consider

- Experiments have shown that bubbles can form in both saline and silicone gel mammary implants but are tolerated quite safely and asymptomatically during normal recreational diving.

- *Decompression stop diving is not recommended for any person fitted with mammary implants.*

MENSTRUAL PERIOD

points to consider

- Many older diving books suggest that there is an increased risk of shark attack (in shark infested waters) whilst diving during the menstrual period. There is absolutely no evidence to support this supposition.

- The average amount of blood lost during an hour's dive whilst menstruating would be only a few millilitres, insufficient to contaminate the sea water, especially if a tampon and wet suit are worn.

- Symptoms during menstruation may include severe abdominal cramping and bloating, headaches and fatigue.

- Symptoms of premenstrual tension may include irritability, lethargy, emotional lability and decreased mental alertness which would interfere with clear thinking.

- Severe fluid retention during the menstrual cycle could theoretically predispose to decompression sickness and difficulty in equalisation of the middle ear, but there is no evidence this occurs.

- *Each female diver should be aware of how she feels during each stage of her menstrual cycle and assess her own ability to dive at that time. In general, there is no reason why a menstruating woman cannot dive.*

SEXUAL INTERCOURSE

Although not relevant specifically to diving, it is a commonly asked question.

points to consider

- The sea and fresh water lakes contain a variety of micro-organisms.
- Sexual intercourse in salt or fresh water will encourage water to enter the vagina and uterus (especially if an intrauterine device is fitted).
- Endometritis and Bartholin's abscesses may result.
- Buoyancy control could be a problem.

- *Safe sexual practices should not be forgotten.*

TAMPONS

points to consider

- Any air space created in the vagina by the insertion of a tampon seems to be insignificant.
- There are no cases of air embolism via the uterus recorded during diving.
- The only recorded cases of air embolism via the uterus are from insufflation of the vagina during oral sex in pregnant women.

Haematology

congenital

ABNORMAL RED CELLS

Spheroctytosis
Elliptocytosis
Ovalocytosis
Stomatocytosis
(NOT sickle cell disease - see later)

point to consider

- Usually cause a mild anaemia but can be normal.

- *If the haemoglobin level is only slightly reduced (say within 2 grams of the normal range) and the diver is otherwise healthy and physically fit, diving may be considered.*

ANAEMIA

Reduction of the red cells in the circulation.

points to consider seriously

- Consider the underlying disease process causing the anaemia.

- Anaemia reduces the oxygen-carrying capacity of the blood and severely reduces exercise tolerance.

- Symptoms include fatigue, tiredness, and dyspnoea.

- Angina, heart failure and confusion can be provoked.

- *Any diver with anaemia should be fully investigated and treated before diving is recommended.*

- *If chronic, diving is not recommended unless the haemoglobin is near normal (within about 2g) and the diver is physically fit and undertakes regular exercise.*

BLEEDING DISORDERS

eg. Haemophilia
Von Willebrand's
** disease**
Thrombocytopaenia
Anticoagulant therapy

points to consider very seriously

- Middle ear barotrauma with haemorrhage is a very common injury whilst scuba diving.

- Minor trauma to the skin is also very common.

- Other barotrauma with minor haemorrhage, especially of the lungs, is probably more common than suspected.

- Neurological decompression sickness (especially of the spinal cord) is often associated with haemorrhage within the neural tissue.

- *Anyone with a bleeding disorder or on anticoagulants is strongly recommended not to dive.*

POLYCYTHAEMIA
polycythaemia vera

Excess red cells in the circulation.

points to consider seriously

- Can be associated with living at high altitude.
- More often it is a symptom of serious disease, especially chronic lung disease, causing chronic hypoxia.
- The increase in red cell density will impair tissue perfusion, predisposing to decompression sickness.
- The expanded blood volume causes an increased cardiac output and decrease in exercise tolerance.
- There is a tendency to increased bleeding.
- *Diving is not recommended.*

SICKLE CELL DISEASE

An inherited "sickle-shaped" red blood cell due to HbS, consisting of 2α and 2 abnormal ß chains.

points to consider very seriously

- More common in divers of negroid race.
- Sickle-shaped red blood cells are more rigid and tend to obstruct capillary blood flow, causing local hypoxia.
- Excessive sickling (leading to a crisis) is aggravated by hypoxia, cold and dehydration.
- A sickle cell crisis causes sudden severe pain, especially in the abdomen, chest and joints, and, rarely, a convulsion or stroke.
- Recurrent vaso-occlusive insults can impair pulmonary function and cause intrapulmonary arterial venous shunting, reducing oxygenation of the blood and reducing the effectiveness of the pulmonary vascular filter.
- Associated with a severe haemolytic anaemia.
- *Diving is contraindicated.*

SICKLE CELL TRAIT

points to consider

- The heterozygous form of sickle cell disease where the blood contains 35-40% HbS and 55-60% of HbA.
- Usually there are few clinical problems.
- Sickle cell crises only occur with very severe hypoxia.
- *Diving may be considered after full discussion about the possible dangers.*

THALASSAEMIA

A deficiency of α or ß chain synthesis.

- Seen frequently in people originating from the Middle and Far East and the Mediterranean.

ß major

points to consider very seriously

- The homozygote form.
- Unable to synthesise HbA.
- Develops severe hypochromic and haemolytic anaemia.
- Causes failure to thrive in childhood.
- Infants who survive develop hepatosplenomegaly, brittle and overgrown long bones.
- Bone marrow transplantation has been used successfully.

- *Diving is contraindicated.*

ß minor

points to consider

- The heterozygotous form.
- Usually asymptomatic.
  Can present as an iron resistant mild hypochromic, microcytic anaemia.
- Diagnosed by finding a raised HbA_2 level 4-7%.

- *If the haemoglobin level is near normal (within 2 grams) diving may be considered.*

Infectious Diseases

points to ponder

- Diving is a social sport sometimes involving close body contact and shared equipment.
- Many infectious diseases are associated with disabling symptoms, such as fever, fatigue, tiredness and vomiting.
- Most infectious diseases are self-limiting or easily treated and will only disqualify a diver for a short period.
- Some infections may be or become chronic. In these cases, the fitness of the diver and the infectivity to other divers must both be considered.
- A few infectious diseases are worthy of individual mention.

AIDS
Acquired immune deficiency syndrome

points to consider very seriously

- AIDS sufferers have a debilitating disease involving fever, weight loss, fatigue and generalised persistent lymphadenopathy.
- There is a greater risk of opportunistic infection, including Pneumocystitis pneumoniae, tuberculosis, viral and fungal.
- Chronic persistent diarrhoea is common.
- *Divers suffering from AIDS are strongly recommended not to dive.*

HIV POSITIVE

points to consider seriously

- Divers who are HIV positive are usually clinically well.
- The AID's virus is only contagious by contact of infected body fluids on broken skin or mucosa.
- The only time that divers would be in contact with other diver's body fluids would be whilst buddy breathing, when there could be an interchange of saliva.
- There are no cases of HIV infection known to have occurred via this route.
- The concentration of infected lymphocytes is far lower in saliva than in blood or semen.
- Additionally, whilst buddy breathing underwater, any saliva on the regulator is diluted by water whilst passing the regulator from diver to diver.
- Infection via saliva would still demand a break in the oral mucosa of the non-infected diver.

- There is controversy over whether cognitive impairment occurs early in HIV disease. Where impairment has been reported, the findings are typically sub clinical, affect only a minority, and their relationship to actual functioning has not been established.
- It has been recommended that HIV positive pilots be disqualified from flying.
- It has been suggested that hyperbaric oxygen could reduce the effectiveness of the blood brain barrier and accelerate the onset of cerebral AIDS.

- *HIV positive divers should avoid buddy breathing and ensure they have an octopus regulator or, even better, another source of air (eg. "Spare Air").*
- *HIV positive divers should ensure their regulators are adequately disinfected after use.*
- *Buddy breathing practice out of the water where the same regulator is used by two divers is not recommended.*
- *HIV positive divers should be warned of the growing evidence of early onset sub-clinical neuro-psychiatric problems and the theoretical concern that diving could accelerate them.*

HEPATITIS B and HEPATITIS C
Chronic active hepatitis Hepatitis B carrier

points to consider seriously

- The acute illness involves lethargy, anorexia, abdominal discomfort, jaundice and hepatomegaly which would make diving quite unsafe.
- Chronic active hepatitis occurs in 1-3% of cases of hepatitis B.
- It is associated with continued abnormal liver function tests and a lack of complete resolution of anorexia, weight loss and fatigue.
- Hepatitis B is a far more virulent and common virus than the AID's virus. Hence, it is more likely to be "caught".
- Carriers of HBsAg are usually quite fit but do shed virus in the saliva.

- *Anyone with an acute or chronic active hepatitis should not dive.*
- *Any carrier of Hepatitis B should not buddy breathe but should carry an octopus regulator or, even better, an alternative air supply (eg. Spare Air).*
- *Any carrier of Hepatitis B should ensure that their regulator is adequately disinfected after use.*
- *Buddy breathing practice out of water is not recommended.*

Recent
INFECTIOUS
MONONUCLEOSIS
Glandular fever

points to consider seriously

- Can have a convalescent period of up to six months.
- Splenomegaly and hepatitis can persist.

■ *Diving is not recommended until full recovery is apparent.*

MALARIA

A protozoan disease transmitted to humans by the bite of the Anopheles mosquito.

points to consider seriously

- Develops within one to six weeks of the original bite.
- Symptoms are characterised by rigors, fever, weakness, jaundice and anaemia.
- Early symptoms can be similar to "flu" and can be confused with early symptoms of decompression illness.
- It has a chronic relapsing course and may recur months or years later.
- Malaria can cause massive splenomegaly.

■ *All divers visiting malarial areas should minimise the risk of malaria by simple self-help measures and by taking prophylactic drugs.*

■ *Mefloquine (Lariam) is best avoided for anti-malarial prophylaxis (See under anti-malarials on Page 51).*

■ *Any diver suffering an attack of malaria is strongly recommended not to dive until it has fully resolved.*

Malignant Disease

Must be evaluated on an individual basis.

points to consider very seriously

1. The debilitating effects of the primary disease.

   Common symptoms include weakness and tiredness, loss of appetite and weight loss.

2. The complications of the primary disease.

   These include:

   - High incidence of depressive illness.
   - Secondary bleeding tendencies (eg. thrombocytopaenia in leukaemia).
   - Anaemia.
   - Susceptibility to secondary infection.
   - Many malignancies (eg. Hodgkin's lymphoma) commonly develop pulmonary infiltrates.
   - Myopathies and Neuropathies.
   - Pulmonary and pericardial effusions.
   - Ascites.

3. The effects and complications of secondary deposits.

4. The effects of treatment.
   - The debilitating effects of major surgery.
   - The side effects of cytotoxic drugs, especially nausea, vomiting, bleeding disorders, pulmonary pneumonitis and fibrosis.
   - The late complications of radiotherapy, especially pneumonitis, pericarditis and myelitis.
   - The very late complications of radiotherapy include fibrosis of soft tissue and lungs within the radiation field, coronary artery disease and pancytopaenia.
   - *Each case must be determined on an individual basis.*
   - *There are many cases of malignant disease where diving is completely safe.*
   - *It is sometimes tempting to override good medical opinion with emotional consideration for the cancer patient who wants to experience diving yet has contraindications. Extreme caution is advised.*

A 42 year old female had a history of a mastectomy for carcinoma of the right breast 1 year previously. Six weeks post operatively she had a course of radiation to the right breast and right axilla. She was now well and playing regular sport. Her lung function was normal but a chest x-ray showed pulmonary apical fibrosis, an expected finding after axillary radiation. She was classed unfit to dive.

Musculoskeletal

points to ponder

- Divers should have the mobility to put on all equipment unassisted, enter the water unassisted, swim unassisted, rescue a buddy, exit the water unassisted and remove all equipment unassisted.
- If unable to do so, special arrangement should be made to assist that diver before diving commences.
- Diving tanks and weight belts are heavy and require some strength to manoeuvre and fit.
- Kitting up is often undertaken in confined spaces on moving boat decks and agility and stability of movement are required.

AMPUTEES

points to consider

- Leg amputees will have some trouble kitting up on boats in rough conditions, any water entry more than a jump, finning and exiting the water.
- Arm amputees will always need assistance to kit up and remove diving equipment.
- Entry and exits can be difficult.
- Both will have difficulty in rescues.

- *Diving may be considered at selected sites if prior arrangements are made, usually including diving in a threesome.*

CERVICAL SPONDYLOSIS

points to consider

- Kitting up may involve extreme movements of the neck, such as looking around for a lost glove when completely kitted up, wearing a mask and sitting in a small boat.
- Diving, especially if buoyancy or centre of gravity is poorly adjusted, may involve swimming "head down" with the neck extended, which can aggravate neck pain.
- Parasthesia of the arms and hands, a common complication of cervical spondylosis, may be confused with decompression illness.

- *Any diver with a history of cervical spondylsis is recommended not to dive while they are suffering neck pain or any acute neurological complication.*
- *The body should be neutrally buoyant and evenly balanced to avoid unnatural finning positions.*

LOW BACK PAIN

"Bad back"
"Disc problems"
Prolapsed intervertebral
 disc
Lumbar spondylosis

points to consider seriously

- Scuba diving involves lifting heavy equipment, kitting up in restricted, awkward spaces and pulling oneself into boats, up ladders and over slippery rocks.
- Once in the water, there is normally no strain on the back. In fact, some divers get relief from their sciatic pain whilst diving.
- Parasthesia and numbness of the legs are common complications of prolapsed intervertebral discs and can be confused with decompression illness.

- *Any diver with acute back pain is recommended not to dive until full normal activity is possible.*
- *All divers with a history of back pain should be warned and reminded of proper lifting techniques, advised to recommence back exercises and to seek help in putting their tanks on.*

Common
FRACTURES
eg. Broken arm or leg

points to consider seriously

- Any fracture will disrupt function and limit mobility.
- Any injured area is possibly more prone to decompression sickness.

- *After any fracture, diving is not recommended for at least twice the period it takes for union. (For the common uncomplicated fractures this approximates twice the length of time the plaster is worn)*

LUMBAR LAMINECTOMY
or Spinal fusion

points to consider seriously

- Having had an operation does not decrease the risks of aggravating the initial back condition.
- The disruption of the paravertebral venous plexus during surgery has been suggested to predispose to spinal decompression sickness. There is no evidence to support this view.

- *Provided spinal movement is adequate and advice on back care as described under "low back pain" is given, diving may be considered.*

A 27 year old Australian male had a rare history of malignant ependoma of the spine. He had had eighteen operations covering the length of his spine to remove a total of 20 tumours over a 10 year period. Both his legs were numb. A recent NMI scan showed no recurrence. Owing to the extensive surgery on his spine with the inevitable scar tissue he was considered high risk for spinal decompression sickness and classed unfit to dive.

ORTHOPAEDIC PINS AND PLATES, JOINT PROSTHESES

points to consider

- Review the original injury or disease necessitating the surgery.

- Ensure function of the body part is compatible with safe diving.

- Hip prostheses are susceptible to dislocation by sudden excessive abduction which could occur by slipping on a wet deck, or whilst manoeuvring weightlessly underwater.

- There is no evidence to suggest that metal or plastic within the body is a focus for bubble formation in decompression sickness.

- *Orthopaedic pins and plates can be ignored as long as function is compatible with safe diving.*

- *Divers with a hip prosthesis should be warned to be cautious and avoid excessive hip abduction.*

PECTUS EXCAVATUM
Funnel chest

Depression of the body of the sternum and xiphoid process combined with inward curving of the costal cartilages and adjacent ribs.

points to consider

- If severe, it can predispose to repeated respiratory infections.

- It can be corrected by surgery, which does not disrupt the visceral pleura.

- *If lung function is normal, diving may be considered.*

PNEUMOCYSTS
(a real rare one)

An air-containing cyst in bone.

points to consider

- Can cause pain on descent.

- Their presence is probably unknown until diving is commenced!

A 42 year old Canadian male had a history of a prolapsed L4/5 intervertebral disc 4 years previously. Whilst lifting his scuba tank over his head he had sudden onset of severe lumbar pain and was unable to move because of the muscle spasm and intense pain. The dive boat had to abort the day's diving and return to the mainland for medical assistance.

TEMPORO-MANDIBULAR DISORDERS and MYOFACIAL PAIN
eg. Temporo-mandibular joint dysfunction syndrome (TMJDS)

points to consider

- Anxiety in divers is often associated with biting hard on the regulator mouthpiece, causing pain in the temporo-mandibular (TM) joint or muscles of the face (especially the masticatory muscles).

- Most commercially available regulator mouthpieces have the interdental bite blocks between the canine and premolar teeth. The lack of posterior support could cause abnormal loads on the myofacial muscles and temporomandibular joint.

- *Anyone with a history of TMJDS or myofacial pain should be advised of the possible aggravation of their condition whilst diving.*

- *Any diver suffering TMJDS or myofacial pain should consider having a custom made mouthpiece, incorporating posterior dental support.*

SCOLIOSIS

Lateral curvature of the spine usually complicated by a rotational deformity which causes asymmetry of the thorax.

points to consider seriously

- Curves greater than 20° may show restriction of pulmonary function.

- Certain surgical procedures (eg. Dwyer's procedure) to correct the deformity use an anterior approach through the thoracic cavity. This will inevitably cause numerous pleural adhesions.

- The alternative surgical procedure, insertion of a Harrington's Rod, takes a posterior approach with no involvement of the pleura.

- *Any diver with severe scoliosis should have regular lung function tests and chest X-rays to monitor the progress of their condition.*

- *Any diver who has had surgical correction involving an anterior approach through the pleural cavity is strongly recommended not to dive.*

A 34 year old Australian female had a long history of myofascial pain and took diazepam and strong analgesics daily. In view of the side effects of her medication and the possible aggravation of her condition she was classed as unfit to dive.

Nervous System

- Diving demands full consciousness, coordinated movement and normal muscle power.
- Any loss or clouding of consciousness whilst diving will quickly result in drowning.
- Decompression sickness commonly affects the nervous system, especially if previously damaged.
- The spinal cord is a specific target organ for decompression sickness.

DEGENERATIVE NERVOUS SYSTEM DISORDERS
eg. Dementia
Motor neurone disease
Parkinson's disease

points to consider very seriously

- Many such conditions will decrease mental alertness, coordination and physical fitness.
- These disorders begin insidiously and run a gradually progressive course; the earliest changes being quite subtle.
- By the time most of these conditions are identified there are significant symptoms which will prove adverse when diving.

- *Diving is contraindicated.*

VENTRICULO-PERITONEAL/ ATRIAL SHUNTS

points to consider seriously

- Usually inserted for hydrocephalus due to congenital abnormalities (eg. aqueduct stenosis) or post natal causes such as meningitis, intracranial haemorrhage or tumour.
- Normal brain development depends on the cause of the obstruction and speed of treatment.
- Low grade infection often prevents the valves from being permanently effective and requires frequent shunt revision.
- There is a concern that an atrial shunt could aggravate bubble formation in supersaturated blood.

- *Diving is not recommended with an atrial shunt.*
- *With a peritoneal shunt, diving may be considered if brain development is normal with no neurological signs or symptoms and the shunt has not needed recent revision.*

BELL'S PALSY

points to consider

- Ensure that the palsy was not due to facial baroparesis. (See Page 118)
- Residual facial weakness may occur.

■ *Diving is not recommended during an acute attack and for at least a month after resolution of all symptoms.*

■ *If facial weakness persists, diving may be considered as long as the regulator mouthpiece can be securely retained in the mouth.*

CHRONIC FATIGUE SYNDROME
Myalgia encephalitis (ME)

points to consider very seriously

Characteristic features include:

- Chronic persisting or relapsing fatigue of a generalised nature, exacerbated by minor exercise.
- Impairment of concentration.
- Short term memory loss.
- Symptoms continue longer than 6 months.

■ *Diving is not recommended whilst fatigue persists.*

EPILEPSY
Febrile convulsion
Neonatal convulsion
Petit mal

Another very controversial issue in diving medicine. Epilepsy is defined as having two or more convulsions.

points to consider very seriously

- A convulsion often reflects a lesion on the brain which is permanent.
- There are some patients in whom the condition is self-limiting (eg. primary generalised epilepsy).
- Even after many convulsion-free years, it is possible to convulse again.
- The relapse rate of epileptics who are taken off medication decreases exponentially, the majority of those relapsing doing so within the first eighteen months and most relapsing within three years.
- People with epilepsy are thought to have a lower seizure threshold.

A 32 year old female had had convulsions since 10 years of age. She took dilantin but had not had a convulsion for 14 years. She drove a car and suffered no apparent side effects from her medication. She did not cease her medication because she did not want to spoil the status quo.

She was classed unfit to dive and advised that if she wanted to dive she should stop medication. If she was fit free, had a normal EEG and was favourably assessed by a neurologist she could then be considered for diving after 3 years.

Epilepsy
(continued)

- Underwater, a diver may be exposed to possible triggering stimuli for convulsions including glare, flickering lights, sensory deprivation and hyperventilation.

- Having a convulsion underwater often involves breath holding during the tonic and clonic phases making pulmonary barotrauma a high risk (as well as drowning).

- People with epilepsy can usually obtain a driver's license if convulsion-free for two years, but cannot get a pilot's or a commercial driver's license.

- Persons with epilepsy are disqualified for military and commercial diving without exception.

- *Many diving doctors would advise that any history of epilepsy should totally disqualify from recreational diving.*

- *Convulsions in early childhood may be acceptable. These would include:*
  - *Neonatal convulsions with no subsequent neurological problems.*
  - *Simple febrile convulsions.*
  - *Convulsions secondary to breath holding attacks.*
  - *Convulsions secondary to drug ingestion.*
  - *Convulsions secondary to sepsis or meningitis with no subsequent neurological problems.*

- *The British Sub Aqua Club Medical Committee recommend that "an epileptic be permitted to dive after five years free from fits and off medication. Where the fits were exclusively nocturnal, this can be reduced to three years."*

- *The Diving Committee of the Underwater Medical Society recommend that "individuals with epilepsy, who have been seizure-free for five years and take no medication, who choose to dive should be advised to avoid hyperventilation and cautioned that elevated pressures of oxygen may precipitate seizures. Individuals with controlled epilepsy (taking medication, seizure free for two years) are advised not to dive."*

---

4) A 29 year old Dutch female had a history of convulsions when three years old. She was on medication for three years and was symptom free until 22 years old when convulsions recurred. She was again on medication for two years but had been free of attacks and off treatment for five years. Due to the recurring nature of her epilepsy she was classed unfit to dive.

HEAD INJURY

**Fractured skull
Unconsciousness
Posttraumatic amnesia
Sub-dural haematoma**

points to consider very seriously

- Head injuries are often associated with brain injury.
- Convulsions can commence following a serious head injury.
- 90% of post-traumatic convulsive disorders become manifest within two years of injury.
- Damaged neurological tissue may be more prone to decompression sickness (DCS).
- Factors that would indicate probable brain injury would include:
  - period of unconsciousness plus post traumatic amnesia longer than 24 hours.
  - epidural, subdural or intracerebral haematoma.
  - convulsion at time or following injury.
  - depressed skull fracture.
  - penetrating head injury.
  - rhinorrhea or otorrhea longer than seven days.
  - post traumatic meningitis or encephalitis.

- *An EEG and full neurological assessment must be performed before diving is considered.*
- *If there are persistent neurological defects, or convulsions have occurred, it is strongly recommended not to dive.*
- *If all is normal, it is recommended not to dive for at least three years and preferably five.*

also consider seriously

- Linear skull fracture with no unconsciousness.
- Unconsciousness and posttraumatic amnesia lasting up to 24 hours.

- *If there is any neurological deficit, it is strongly recommended not to dive.*
- *If neurological assessment is normal, it is recommended not to dive for 2 years.*

and

- Even lesser head injuries with amnesia and/or unconsciousness lasting less than 10 minutes and no neurological sequelae, diving is not recommended for three months.

A 29 year old American male showed no relevant medical history on his diving medical questionnaire. During the examination a scar was noted behind the left ear. Subsequent palpation of the scalp identified numerous irregularities. When further questioned he admitted having had a motor bike accident two years previously in which he had sustained a compound depressed fracture of the skull. He had been unconscious for five weeks and had had several convulsions, the last one eight months previously. He lied on his medical form because he wanted to dive whatever the risk. Because the risk of further convulsions was significant he was classed unfit to dive. The diver was very angry.

INTRACRANIAL HAEMORRHAGE
**Subarachnoid
haemorrhage
Stroke
Cerebral vascular
accident (CVA)**

points to consider very seriously

- Such a bleed reflects either structural or pathological changes in the cerebral circulation.
- There is a high risk of a recurrent bleed.
- After a stroke, there is a 5% per year chance of another stroke and a 5% per year chance of a myocardial infarct.
- Convulsions can commence after such haemorrhages.
- Permanent neurological deficits are common.

- *Diving is contraindicated.*

INTRACRANIAL SURGERY

Full details of surgery performed should first be obtained.

points to consider very seriously

- Any intracranial surgery must leave scar tissue on or in the brain.
- Convulsions can commence after such surgery.
- Many patients are left with permanent neurological deficits.
- Damaged neurological tissue may be more prone to decompression sickness.

- *Diving is not usually recommended.*

MIGRAINE
Cluster headaches

- About 10% of sports divers indicate a history of migraine or severe headaches on their questionnaire.
- Any such history needs to be fully elucidated.

points to consider very seriously

- Symptoms of which to be wary include:
  - Recent frequent attacks (more than one per month)
  - Use of prophylactic medication.
  - Sudden onset of an aura with disabling or neurological symptoms.
  - Sudden onset of vomiting.
  - Severe muscular weakness.
  - Any clouding of consciousness, vertigo, diplopia or slurred speech.
  - Migraine aggravated by swimming, cold or scuba diving.

- *Any such symptom could make diving dangerous and it is strongly recommended not to dive.*

A 24 year old Swiss female had a history of frequent migraines which began suddenly with a visual scotomata and developed into a severe headache often associated with paraesthesia of the left hand and arm. Because of the frequency, suddenness and severity of her symptoms she was classed unfit to dive.

other points to consider seriously

- Other symptoms to ask for would include:
  - – Paraesthesia
  - – Visual disturbances
  - – Mild muscular weakness

- *Since these could be confused with decompression illness, the diver should be warned of the implications, possible expenses and inconveniences.*
- *If attacks are infrequent with no disabling symptoms, diving may be considered.*
- *All divers with a history of migraine should be warned not to dive if they suspect an attack could be starting, and to avoid decompression stop diving, deep diving and always add a safety decompression stop on all dives.*

MUSCULAR DYSTROPHY

Myotonic dystrophy
Becker muscular
dystrophy
Erb's Adult muscular
dystrophy

Progressive hereditary degenerative diseases of skeletal muscle.

points to consider very seriously

- Childhood forms of the dystrophia will be very severely handicapped by adolescence and obviously not fit to dive.
- Those forms with a later onset will still have significant muscular weakness and unlikely to have the necessary strength to scuba dive.
- Many patients are subject to myotonia (ie. prolonged contraction of certain muscles, especially the hands and tongue).

- *Diving is contraindicated.*

MYASTHENIA GRAVIS

Episodic muscular
weakness

A disease of fluctuant weakness of certain voluntary muscles.

points to consider very seriously

- Repeated or persistent activity of a muscle group exhausts its contracting power leading to a progressive weakness.
- Remission may occur but is usually short lived.

- *Diving is not recommended.*

MULTIPLE SCLEROSIS
MS
Demyelinative diseases

Characterised by episodes of focal disorder of the optical nerves, spinal cord and brain which remit to a varying extent and recur over a period of years.

points to consider very seriously

- A common disease with a tendency to attack young people. (Incidence 1 in 800).

- Diagnosis may be uncertain at the onset and awaits development of more characteristic symptoms and signs.

- Initial manifestations are often optic neuritis, ataxia, nystagmus and brainstem signs such as diplopia, vertigo, vomiting and disorders in micturition.

- Other symptoms include weakness, paraesthesia, impaired vision, dysarthria, intention tremor, impairment of deep sensation, parapesis and alteration in emotional response.

- The most common symptom is fatigue.

- About half of these patients present as an intermittently progressive disease.

- A relapse is not usually a sudden event but comes on over hours to days.

- The susceptibility of demyelinated nervous tissue to decompression sickness is not known.

- The symptoms of multiple sclerosis often mimic those of decompression illness. Any such symptom which occurs within days of a dive must be assumed to be decompression illness and treated as such.

- *Many diving doctors would recommend that anyone with confirmed multiple sclerosis or who has had symptoms suggestive of multiple sclerosis, such as optic neuritis within the past year, should not dive.*

- *Some diving doctors would consider anyone with multiple sclerosis who has mild, non-disabling symptoms which have been stable for several years to be fit to dive.*

- *Such divers should avoid decompression stop diving, deep diving and always add a safety decompression stop on all dives.*

- *Even if considered fit to dive, annual reassessments are recommended.*

PARAPLEGIA

Paraplegia is not compatible with routine safe recreational diving. Many paraplegics have dived on special courses or by private arrangement.

This section is included for general interest.

points to consider seriously

- Damaged neurological tissue may be more prone to decompression sickness.
- The spinal cord is especially prone to decompression sickness.
- *Paraplegic divers must therefore accept such risks and dive very conservative dive profiles. There are recorded cases of decompression illness in such divers, even after short shallow dives.*

other points to consider should such risks be acceptable

- Must be a good swimmer.
- The disability should not have been caused by a spinal bend, arteriovenous malformation or transverse myelitis.
- Lung function must be normal. This will limit the level of the lesion to T8 or below. (In marginal cases, lung function can be further reduced in a tight wet suit jacket).
- Skin must be in good condition.
- Good control of urine and bowel movements is essential (with or without artificial aids).
- Kitting up in wet suits can be very difficult.
- Legs trailing in the water are subject to trauma.
- Spasticity of the legs may increase with cold.

SPINAL CORD DISEASE

Brown-Sequard Syndrome
Guillain-Barré Syndrome
Spinal cord trauma

points to consider seriously

- The spinal cord is especially subject to decompression sickness (DCS).
- Damaged neural tissue may be more vulnerable to decompression sickness.
- Divers with a history of spinal cord disease may have a reduced reserve functional capacity, so any subsequent damage by DCS will be more severe.

- *If a permanent neurological deficit remains, diving is not recommended.*
- *If no neurological deficit exists, diving may be considered. The possible increased risk for spinal DCS and its possible greater clinical manifestation (because of the lack of reserve function) must be clearly explained to the diver.*
- *Such divers should avoid decompression stop diving, deep diving and always add a safety stop on every dive.*

TRANSIENT ISCHAEMIC ATTACK (TIA)

point to consider very seriously

- A TIA is a marker of cerebral vascular disease.

- *Diving is contraindicated.*

TRIGEMINAL NEURALGIA

point to consider

- A trigger zone on the face can easily be irritated by wearing a mask.

A 23 year old Swedish male had had a motor bike injury 5 years previously when he avulsed 2 cervical nerve roots resulting in permanent weakness and some numbness in his right arm. There had been no associated head or neck injury. Clinically he had sufficient strength in the arm to lift scuba tanks. Being a peripheral nerve injury the danger of spinal decompression sickness was not considered to be increased and he was classed fit to dive.

A 25 year old Australian female had a history of Guillain-Barré Syndrome 10 years previously. She had been mechanically ventilated for 2 weeks and had made a full recovery. Examination, lung function tests and chest X-ray were clear and she was classed fit to dive.

Psychological/Psychiatric

points to ponder

- It seems impossible to assess "psychological suitability" during the course of a single encounter with a diver. But one has to try . . . so closely observe attitudes, reactions and behaviour.
- Scuba diving requires clear thinking, controlled reactions and common sense.
- Anyone lacking any of these is not suited to diving.
  - Clear thinking is clouded by psychosis, neurosis and drugs.
  - Controlled reactions are confused by fear and phobias, (and lack of training).
  - Commonsense is uncommon in the child, the "Cowboy" and the conceited.

BEWARE CERTAIN PERSONALITIES

THE COWBOY

points to consider
- High risk taker.
- Usually male, 18-25 years of age and will scoff at advice given.

THE RELUCTANT BUDDY

- Usually (but not always) a female diver learning to dive to please the male partner.

points to consider seriously
- High level of anxiety evident during the medical.
- If suspicious, ask outright the motive for diving.

- *Avoid allowing partners to have their medicals together.*
- *Dissuade from diving or find convenient physical reason not to dive.*

THE GROUPIE
The runt!

- Seen in groups of young travellers who all do a diving course together but where one of the group is less co-ordinated, less strong and less enthusiastic but who tries to keep up with the rest. Usually a male with no physical reason to fail a medical but who will often have difficulties, especially during open water dives.

- *There is little one can do to prevent them diving.*

A family of four, a father and mother, 15 year old son and 13 year old daughter came together for their diving medical. During the mother's medical it became obvious that she was a reluctant diver and when directly asked her motivation to dive she admitted that she did not really want to dive but was doing it to make it a family activity. She decided not to dive and the daughter readily joined her as she too was "not keen".

ANOREXIA NERVOSA
Bulimia

Pathologically excessive dieting

points to consider very seriously

- Most patients suffering from anorexia nervosa deny the severity of their illness and are brought to treatment by distraught parents or friends.
- A long term mortality of 20% has been reported.
- Despite emaciation most patients are not seriously physically ill.
- Commonly involves excessive preoccupation with food, feelings of inadequacy, anxiety, depression, poor concentration.
- Poor nutrition causes fatigue, hypothermia, hypotension, disturbed blood chemistry, sinus bradycardia.
- Often associated with bulimia involving induced vomiting, laxative and diuretic abuse causing hypokalaemia.

- *Any diver with anorexia nervosa or bulimia or a recent history of them is strongly recommended not to dive until normal nutrition and a body mass index greater than 18 has been attained.*

ANXIETY
Post traumatic stress disorders, Obsessive-compulsive disorders

points to consider seriously

- Small amounts of anxiety are adaptive and offer a normal response.
- In large amounts it is disabling.
- Symptoms include fatigue, tachycardia, light headedness, difficulty in concentration and irritability.
- Treatment often includes tranquillisers.

- *If symptoms are disabling, diving is contraindicated.*
- *Anyone on tranquillisers is strongly recommended not to dive.*

DEPRESSION

points to consider very seriously

- Symptoms include fatigue, slow thinking, poor concentration, recurrent thoughts of death.
- Often treated with antidepressant drugs.
- Can be associated with other serious diseases (eg. malignancy).

- *If actively depressed, under treatment or there is a history of recurrent depressive illness, diving is contraindicated.*

MANIA
Bipolar disorder

points to consider very seriously

- An episodic disorder often interspersed with bouts of depression.
- Attacks usually recur at ever decreasing intervals.
- Symptoms include elevated, expansive mood, physical restlessness, flights of ideas, inflated self esteem (often delusional), excessive involvement in activities that have a high potential for painful consequences.

- *Anyone with even a distant history of mania is strongly recommended not to dive.*
- *Diving is contraindicated for anyone with recent bout of mania, or under treatment.*

PANIC ATTACK

Sudden unexpected and often overwhelming feeling of terror or apprehension.

points to seriously consider

- Often accompanied by symptoms such as shortness of breath, palpitations and faintness.
- Symptoms can peak in less than 10 mins and resolve in 20-30 mins.
- The attacks may be aggravated by a specific situation (eg. work or domestic stresses).
- Can easily (and often does) lead to panic.
- Usually treated with antidepressant or tranquilliser drugs.
- Relapse of panic attacks is common.

- *Anyone with a recent history (within two years) of panic attacks is strongly recommended not to dive.*
- *Anyone with a past history of panic attacks should be warned of the consequences of panic underwater.*

PERSONALITY DISORDERS

point to consider

- A wide range of presentations is possible.

- *Diving is not recommended only if a personality disorder becomes disabling or obviously dangerous.*

A 28 year old Dutch male had a history of taking amphetamines at the age of 16 years. He had become aggressive and paranoid and had required a short hospital admission. He had since had no subsequent psychiatric history and had taken no further drugs. As his psychotic episode had an obvious precipitant which could be and had been well avoided he was classed fit to dive.

PHOBIAS

Extreme distress when confronted with the phobic stimulus.

point to consider seriously

● Most phobias will be unrelated to diving.

The ones to consider include:

Agoraphobia

A fear of wide open spaces

points to consider seriously

● Whilst diving in deep water it is not uncommon to be suspended in midwater, unable to see the surface or the bottom.

● A diver can become disorientated and feels isolated, the so called "blue orb" or "blue dome" syndrome. (It could be aggravated by nitrogen narcosis)

■ *Severe agoraphobics are strongly recommended not to dive.*

■ *Mild cases must be warned to avoid diving in deep water and keep close to the buddy.*

Claustrophobia

A fear of enclosed spaces.

points to consider seriously

● About two percent of sports divers admit to some degree of claustrophobia.

● Underwater feels like an enclosed space.

● It is very enclosed at night.

● It becomes darker with depth.

● Water visibility can reduce suddenly and severely even in apparent ideal conditions.

● A common fear is of being grabbed from below by some large life form.

● The usual reaction to claustrophobia underwater is to escape as quickly as possible to the surface (with the risk of pulmonary barotrauma of ascent).

● Claustrophobia can complicate treatment in hyperbaric chambers, especially small transportable chambers. Heavy sedation may be required.

■ *If severe, diving is contraindicated.*

■ *If mild and the diver is highly motivated, warn of the dangers and advise shallow diving in clear waters and no night diving.*

■ *Wearing a silicone mask allows more light around the eyes and slightly reduces the "hemmed in" feeling.*

Herpetophobia

A fear of snakes.

■ *Such divers should not dive in areas frequented by sea snakes.*

SCHIZOPHRENIA

Schizophrenform disorder

points to consider very seriously

● Affects one percent of the population.

● Symptoms include bizarre illusion, hallucination, markedly illogical thinking, inappropriate reactions.

● Many such patients will be on long term drug treatment.

■ *Diving is contraindicated.*

An 18 year old British female had suffered from panic attacks three years previously. She had taken anafranil for a year. She was now on no medication and had only suffered one mild attack in the previous year. In view of the disastrous consequences of panic attacks whilst diving, the recent history and the likelihood of relapse she was classed unfit to dive.

A 44 year old American backpacking around Australia was taking a MAOI antidepressant for a "sugar addiction". He had also had an "alcohol addiction that was now well controlled". He had taken a year off to readjust his life. During the medical he was very talkative and analytical about every detail. In view of the side effects of the antidepressant and the history suggestive of alcohol abuse associated with a depressive illness he was classed unfit to dive.

A 22 year old English female burst out crying on walking into the consulting room. She was very tired after spending 40 hours on a bus and she was feeling very homesick. She was advised to go and sleep and have a few days relaxation before contemplating a dive course. Diving requires a clear head and should not be undertaken by anyone who is emotionally upset or labile.

A 26 year old American female gave a history of claustrophia. Her boyfriend had told her that she would manage easily underwater. On further questioning she described how she felt uneasy in any room when anybody stood between her and the door. In airliners she felt panicky when everyone stood up to disembark, blocking the aisle. She even felt uneasy when she was in the "middle of America" away from the coast. The normal reaction of a diver panicking is to ascend to the surface as quickly as possible with little thought about exhaling with the great risk of barotrauma of the lung of ascent. She was classed unfit to dive.

A 42 year old Frenchman came to Australia to dive the Great Barrier Reef. He "splashed out" on a week's dive trip to the Swain Reefs, 160 kilometers (100 miles) offshore. On arrival he discovered that the Swain Reef is one of the few reefs that abound with sea snakes. Having a herpetophobia he was unable to leave the boat even to snorkel.

A 26 year old Australian male gave no history of any psychiatric problems. During the course of the medical he behaved in a strange manner and when questioned again about his past history became very aggressive and threatening, accusing the examiner of being "like the rest of them". His general practitioner was contacted and it was discovered that he was a paranoid schizophrenic who had recently stopped his treatment and left home. He was classed unfit to dive.

Respiratory

- Normal lung function is necessary to sustain exercise underwater.
- The lungs (or rather the pulmonary vasculature) act as a filter for any bubbles found in the venous circulation.
- Any air trapping in the lung will cause hyperinflation of the distal lung segment on ascent.
- Barotrauma can occur with hyperinflation of lung tissue.
- Any lung tissue which is fibrotic or scarred will have reduced compliance and its interface with normal lung tissue will tend to tear more easily on hyperinflation.
- The lungs can be safely squeezed until the lung volume is equal to the dead space. Then compensating mechanisms must occur or internal haemorrhage will occur.
- The lung must be able to tolerate rapid changes in volume and pressure.
- Pulmonary barotrauma has been shown to occur with transpulmonary pressure gradients of about 75cm of water.
- Pulmonary barotrauma of ascent is the most dramatic and serious injury encountered by divers.
- Underwater there is a pressure gradient between the apices and bases of the lungs, especially in the vertical position with a shift in the lung volume from the bases to the apex.
- The density of a gas increases with pressure. The deeper one dives, the denser the gas one breathes, the greater the respiratory effort required, especially if respiratory rate and volume are increased with exercise.

ASTHMA
Reactive airways disease
Bronchospasm

Probably the most contentious issue in diving medicine.

An acute, reversible, spasmodic diffuse airway narrowing with persistent reactivity.

points to consider very seriously

- The major concerns are that the asthmatic diver could develop bronchospasm whilst diving and is at risk of pulmonary barotrauma, even on a normal ascent.
- Underwater the diver is exposed to many factors which may precipitate bronchial spasm:
  1. cold air
  2. dry air
  3. exercise
  4. anxiety with hyperventilation
  5. possible inhalation of salt water (hypertonic saline)
- Factors 3, 4 and 5 do not occur until something else starts to go wrong.

- Asthmatics can have non-communicating air spaces even on full inspiration.
- Bronchodilator drugs may leave patchy obstruction within the bronchial tree.
- Bronchodilator drugs given before a dive may lose their full effect before the end of a dive.
- Bronchodilator drugs may concomitantly relax the pulmonary vasculature, reducing the efficiency of the pulmonary vascular filter effect and so increasing the likelihood of decompression sickness.
- Resolved childhood asthma can recur in later life.
- There are numerous anecdotal series of asthmatic diving catastrophes.
- Asthma was a major contributing factor in 8% of diving deaths in Australia and New Zealand in 1980-87.
- One British study of diving asthmatics showed no apparent risk of decompression illness but an American survey suggested a four-fold risk increase.
- A risk assessment of asthma for cerebral arterial gas embolism, made by the Divers Alert Network (DAN), suggested a two-fold increased risk. However, numbers were not statistically significant.

- *The British Sub-Aqua Club recommend that: "diving is permitted by asthmatics if they have allergic asthma, but not if they have exercise, cold or emotion induced asthma. Asthmatics may dive if their symptoms are controlled by Intal plain (but not compound) and/or inhaled steroids . . . Asthmatics may also dive if they only occasionally need to take bronchodilators . . . An asthmatic who infrequently needs bronchodilators and who is permitted to dive should not do so or if he/she has needed to take a bronchodilator in the 48 hours preceding the dive or if he/she has any wheeze or other chest symptom at the time of the dive."*

A 23 year old German male gave a history of childhood asthma until the age of 9 years. He had been hospitalised several times as a child but had had no symptoms or medication since. His lung function and examination was normal but when given a hypertonic saline test his FEV_1 dropped 33% within one minute and he became severely wheezy requiring nebulised salbutamol. When he realised that this could possibly occur underwater he decided not to scuba dive. He was a classed unfit to dive.

A 25 year old British male ticked the "yes" box for asthma and wheezing. He had never had asthma but had been told that whenever he consumed a lot of alcohol he wheezed when he was asleep. He had never wheezed whilst he was sober and had never used a bronchodilator inhaler. The rest of his medical was normal. His lung function and a hypertonic saline provocation test were both normal. His "wheeze" was not considered asthmatic in nature and he was classed fit to dive.

Asthma
(continued)

■ *The Thoracic Society of Australia and New Zealand made an extensive review of "compressed air diving and respiratory disease". It recommended:*

"those who have had asthma in the past, but who have normal spirometric tests and no symptoms, and have not taken asthma medication at all in the last five years, should proceed to bronchial provocation testing . . . if bronchial hyperresponsiveness is present, subjects should not be passed fit to dive. It should be accepted, however, that at present the recommendation against diving for subjects with bronchial hyperresponsiveness and past asthma is made on theoretical grounds. There are sound reasons to suggest that, along with current asthmatics, such divers have an increased risk of pulmonary barotrauma or arterial gas embolism, but at present there are insufficient data to confirm or refute this".

BRONCHIAL CARCINOMA
Lung cancer

points to consider very seriously

● Any tumour of the bronchus will involve disruption of the lung's architecture.

● Surgical or radiation therapy will only further disrupt the architecture.

■ *Diving is contraindicated because of the increased risks of pulmonary barotrauma.*

CHEST WALL INJURIES
**Crushed chest
Multiple rib fractures**

points to consider seriously

● Usually associated with a traumatic penetrating pneumothorax.

● High probability of scarring to pleural and peripheral lung tissue.

● Treatment may have involved mechanical ventilation of the lungs.

■ *It is strongly recommended not to dive if a chest wall injury involves damage to the underlying lung tissue, because the subsequent scarring of the lung and pleura may increase the risk of pulmonary barotrauma.*

A 23 year old British female had no significant past medical history except that she had become wheezy during a steep mountain walk two years previously. Lung function and examination were normal. She was given a hypertonic saline provocation test when her FEV_1 dropped 40% within two minutes. It was considered that a combination of exercise and inhaling cold air (a common combination whilst diving) was bronchoconstricting and she was classed unfit to dive.

A 54 year old Australian non smoking male had a history of inoperable bronchial carcinoma. He had had a course of radiotherapy and had been told by his oncologist that there was no reason that he could not dive. He was feeling very fit, walking ten kilometers a day, taking large doses of vitamins and meditating daily. A chest X-ray confirmed a large left sided hilar mass with extensive fibrosis and he was classed unfit to dive. He was disappointed mainly because his expectations were so high but was happy not to dive when the dangers were explained.

EMPHYSEMA

Chronic airways disease
Chronic bronchitis
Chronic obstructive
airways disease
(COAD)

Emphysema is characterised by abnormal enlargement of the air spaces distal to the terminal bronchioles, with destruction of alveolar walls.

Chronic bronchitis is characterised by increased mucus producing cells in the walls of the bronchi and bronchioles.

points to consider very seriously

- Increased mucus production creates mucus plugs that cause air trapping in distal lung.
- Destruction of alveoli leads to the formation of bullae.
- Diagnosis is usually made from a history of cough, recurrent chest infections and shortness of breath.
- Lung function tests will show a reduction in FEV1 greater than in FVC with a reduced ratio.

- *Diving is contraindicated because of the severe risks of pulmonary barotrauma.*

EXTRINSIC ALLERGIC ALVEOLITIS

eg. Farmer's lung
Bird fancier's lung
Mushroom worker's
lung
Thatched roof lung
Pituitary snuff taker's
lung
Woodworker's lung

A chronic inflammatory disease of the lung resulting from sensitisation and subsequent exposure to a variety of organic dusts.

points to consider very seriously

- An acute attack causes fever, dyspnoea at rest, inspiratory crackles but no rhonchi.
- Chest X-ray shows diffuse micronodular shadowing.
- Both FVC and FEV1 drop with a normal ratio.
- As few as 5 acute symptomatic recurrences can have significantly reduced lung function.
- The chronic form is often progressive and may result in progressive respiratory failure.

- *Diving is not recommended for at least four weeks after an acute attack.*
- *Anyone with a history of recurrent attacks should be fully assessed by a respiratory physician to exclude pulmonary fibrosis before diving is considered.*

A 27 year old male Canadian gave no significant past medical history on his questionnaire or at the interview. His FVC was noted to be only 63% of predicted and his FEV_1 only 73% of predicted even on retest. He suggested this might be due to the collapsed lung he had when he was a baby. A subsequent chest X-ray showed severe fibrosis and pleural adhesions on the right side. He was classed unfit to dive.

A 35 year old British male, a farmer, gave a history of "farmer's lung" aggravated when cutting hay. He had had two occurrences, the last one two years previously. He had changed his farming practices and no longer cut hay.

He was otherwise well. His lung function and chest X-ray were normal and he was classed fit to dive.

PLEURAL ADHESIONS
Intrathoracic surgery

points to consider seriously

- Pleural adhesions will tether lung tissue to the chest wall, reducing its elasticity.
- Tethered lung tissue will tear at lesser degrees of overinflation than normal lung tissue.
- Diaphragmatic pleural adhesions have been demonstrated to cause more pulmonary barotrauma than pleural adhesions to the chest wall.

- *Any diver with pleural adhesions demonstrable on chest X-ray or with a history of intrathoracic surgery is recommended not to dive.*

PLEURODESIS PLEURECTOMY

points to consider very seriously

- Commonly performed for recurrent spontaneous pneumothoraces.
- There is a recurrence rate of 8% following pleurodesis.
- Recurrence is rare following pleurectomy.
- Even if recurrence of pneumothorax is not possible, the underlying cystic lung disease probably remains, with the inherent danger now being an air embolus.

- *It is strongly recommended not to dive.*

PNEUMOCONIOSES
**eg. Silicosis
Coal worker's pneumoconiosis
Talcosis
Asbestosis
Volcanic ash lung!**

Lung disease caused by mineral dust.

points to consider very seriously

- Dust particle irritation causes pulmonary fibrosis.
- In early stages there are no symptoms despite X-ray changes.
- In coal miners progressive massive fibrosis may occur with cavitation.
- Asbestos exposure can cause benign pleural effusions, calcified pleural plaques, asbestosis and mesothelioma.

- *Diving is contraindicated due to the high risk of pulmonary barotrauma.*

A 26 year old Australian male had had an spontaneous pneumothorax 2 years previously requiring admission to hospital. No chest drain had been inserted and it had been resorbed spontaneously. He had then had a high definition CAT scan of his lungs which had shown no abnormalities and he had decided to continue diving. On his 20th subsequent dive he had made a rapid ascent in aid of his buddy. Immediately on the surface he felt right sided chest pain and breathless. His buddy towed him to the boat and he was evacuated to the mainland where a chest X-ray confirmed a pneumothorax. He was hospitalised and given 100% oxygen. The pneumothorax was resorbed without the need for a chest drain. He decided not to dive again!

PNEUMOTHORAX

points to consider very seriously

- A primary spontaneous pneumothorax usually reflects underlying cystic lung disease.
- There is a recurrence rate of 33-50%.
- A secondary spontaneous pneumothorax is caused by many diseases affecting the lung (eg. asthma, scleroderma, tuberous sclerosis). The most common underlying cause is chronic obstructive pulmonary disease.
- Perforating chest injuries causing a traumatic pneumothorax by penetration of lung tissue will leave scar tissue on the lung and pleural adhesions.
- Blunt non-penetrating injuries to the chest causing a pneumothorax (eg. a karate chop), and iatrogenic pneumothoraces from needles (eg. CVP lines), are not associated with significant lung scarring.
- Pneumothorax is a common complication of mechanical ventilation of the lungs due to the reduced compliance of diseased lungs and the higher pressures used during ventilation.
- A pneumothorax occurring underwater will increase in size on ascent, causing tension.

- *A spontaneous pneumothorax, whether primary or secondary, is a contraindication to diving.*
- *It is strongly recommended not to dive following a traumatic pneumothorax which penetrates and disrupts lung tissue.*
- *Diving may be considered following a traumatic pneumothorax which does not involve penetration of the lung tissue, or an iatrogenic pneumothorax from a needle or mechanical ventilation, providing a chest X-ray is completely normal. Sufficient time (at least three months) must be allowed for adequate healing.*
- *The possible risks and dangers of pneumothoraces should be fully explained to the diver.*

PULMONARY ARTERIOVENOUS FISTULA
eg. Rendu Osler Weber disease
Anomalous pulmonary venous drainage

points to consider very seriously

- The pulmonary vascular bed acts as a filter for air bubbles in the venous circulation.
- Any arterio-venous fistula will bypass this filter and allow bubbles to enter the arterial vasculature.
- This will predispose to arterial gas embolism.

- *Diving is contraindicated.*

PULMONARY EMBOLUS

points to consider seriously

- If no infarction has occurred, only haemorrhage, the architecture and structure of the lung are preserved. Resolution will lead to almost completely normal tissue.
- If infarction occurs, the lung will be scarred and pleural adhesions may be present.

▪ *If the chest X-ray is normal, diving may be considered.*

▪ *In doubtful cases consider a V/Q scan. If normal, residual damage is most unlikely.*

SHOCK LUNG

Adult respiratory distress syndrome ARDS

Acute, progressive respiratory failure following severe trauma.

points to consider seriously

- Even after apparent recovery, reduced lung compliance can continue.
- Maximal improvement in lung function may take six months.
- Pulmonary fibrosis can occur.

▪ *Full specialist respiratory assessment is advisable before diving is recommended.*

SARCOIDOSIS

A multisystem granulomatous disease of unknown origin that commonly affects the lung.

points to consider seriously

- 80% of cases occur between 20 and 45 years of age.
- Pulmonary sarcoid can be symptomless and only found on routine chest X-ray.
- Abnormalities on chest X-ray, including intrathoracic lymphadenopathy and parenchymal infiltrates, are present in 90-95% of cases.
- Pulmonary function tests are usually normal if there is no parenchymal infiltration on chest X-ray.
- Spontaneous remission occurs in two thirds of patients. Ninety per cent of patients with radiographic Stage 1 disease spontaneously remit.
- Eighty five per cent of remissions occur within the first two years.

▪ *Active sarcoidosis is a contraindication to diving.*

▪ *Any diver with a history of sarcoid should have a full respiratory assessment to exclude pulmonary fibrosis before diving is recommended.*

▪ *Any diver with a history of sarcoid is recommended to have an annual medical.*

TRACHEOSTOMY
now closed

points to consider

- Assess whether the reason for the tracheostomy will be a danger to diving (eg. a history of a crushed chest).
- Note any stenosis of the trachea.
- Usually it is not upper airway resistance that is the limiting factor for expiratory flow rates. A slightly narrowed trachea will not be a risk factor for pulmonary barotrauma.
- *Diving may be considered.*

A 25 year old Danish male had had recurrent pneumonia as a child and had a right lower lobectomy at the age of 11 years. He smoked 20 cigarettes a day and was noted to have bronchitis when examined. As his chest surgery with the subsequent fibrotic scarring would increase the risk of pulmonary barotrauma he was classed unfit to dive. He was very upset because he had had a "resort course" the day before "without mishap".

A 44 year old British male had a history of a DVT caused after an injury to his leg ten years previously. Despite being anticoagulated he had a pulmonary embolus from which he made an uneventful recovery. Examination, lung function and chest X-ray were all normal and he was classed fit to dive.

A 40 year old Frenchman had a history of sarcoidosis five years before. He had been dyspnoeic and chest X-ray had shown bilateral hilar lymphadenopathy with fine pulmonary reticular-nodular shadowing (Stage 2). He had been treated with corticosteroids. He was now symptomless but his chest X-ray still showed some fine shadowing. He was classed unfit to dive.

A 33 year old Australian had a history of sarcoidosis ten years before. He had presented with erythema nodosum and chest X-ray had shown bilateral hilar lymphadenopathy (Stage 1). He received no treatment and after one year his chest X-ray was normal. He had remained well and all follow up chest X-rays, including one the previous month, were clear. He was classed fit to dive but advised to have annual medicals.

Surgery

HERNIA OF ABDOMINAL WALL

eg. **Inguinal hernia**
Incisional hernia
Umbilical hernia
Femoral hernia

points to consider very seriously

- Lifting heavy equipment (eg. tanks) will aggravate the hernia.
- If the hernia contains any intestine, air "trapping" could lead to overdistension and strangulation, or even rupture, during ascent.

- *Diving is not recommended until after repair of the hernia.*

KIDNEY TRANSPLANT

points to consider

- The transplanted kidney is situated in the lower abdomen.
- Blood pressure may be elevated or controlled with anti-hypertensive drugs.
- Renal function may be compromised.
- The usual immunosuppressant drugs azathioprine, prednisolone and cyclosporin have no known adverse side effects for diving.
- It takes about a year following surgery to assess fully the result of a transplant.

- *If renal function and blood pressure are normal, diving may be considered a year after surgery.*

Recent abdominal SURGERY

points to consider

- Scars need to be fully healed to avoid infection.
- Abdominal muscles need to be fully healed before heavy lifting is safe.

- *An increasing exercise program should be undertaken before starting diving.*
- *A minimum of six week's delay post operatively is recommended.*
- *Early dives should be easy and shallow.*

A renal surgeon issued a "fitness to dive" certificate to his patient who had had a renal transplant eighteen months previously. He endorsed it by adding that because the transplanted kidney was in the lower abdomen it was "now subject to pressure" and the diver should not dive to more than 10m (33ft) for 20 minutes! (See Pascal's Principle on Page 3.)

Diving Accidents

DECOMPRESSION SICKNESS

Decompression illness

points to consider very seriously

- The only way to be certain to avoid decompression sickness is either not to dive or not to ascend.
- If the dive profile of the dive(s) leading up to the decompression sickness (DCS) was well within the limits of the dive tables, it may be that the diver is susceptible to DCS and runs a high risk of recurrence.
- If the diver has had more than one episode of DCS it might reflect a greater susceptibility to DCS, or a lack of awareness or responsibility in dive planning.
- If there is any residual neurological defect following DCS, the diver runs a greater risk of further and more severe neurological DCS.

- *All divers suffering DCS should be investigated for predisposing causes (eg. patent foramen ovale) and be followed up clinically for at least a year.*

- *Even with apparent full recovery after initial treatment, it is strongly recommended not to dive for at least a month.*

- *All remediable risk factors should be corrected (eg. reduce weight if obese, increase physical fitness, avoidance of dehydration).*

- *All future diving should have more conservative dive profiles by reducing the no-stop times and ascent rates and avoiding decompression stop dives, repetitive dives and deep dives.*

- *Even if mild neurological sequelae exist, as long as they are stable and the diver is physically and psychologically fit, diving to 9 metres (30 ft) for short periods may be considered after one year.*

- *Inner ear decompression sickness (a very rare event in recreational diving) with any evidence of residual damage to the cochlear or vestibular apparatus should preclude future diving.*

A 22 year old diving instructor developed left knee pain and paraesthesia in his right foot following a conservative dive profile. He had a history of a previous episode of musculoskeletal decompression illness. He was recompressed with full resolution of his symptoms but advised not to dive again. To have two episodes of DCI whilst diving within conservative dive profiles is strong evidence of a susceptibility to DCI.

FACIAL BAROPARESIS

A temporary facial nerve palsy caused by pressure on the facial nerve through a bony defect of the facial nerve canal in the middle ear when the middle ear is subject to poor equalisation.

points to consider seriously

- Will most probably recur.
- The nerve palsy can become permanent.
- *It is strongly recommended not to dive.*

PULMONARY BAROTRAUMA
Arterial gas embolism (A.G.E.)
Pneumothorax
Cervical and Mediastinal emphysema

points to consider very seriously

- Pulmonary barotrauma is caused by over inflation of the lungs.
- The overinflation will be due to either a sudden rapid ascent with inadequate air venting (a so called "deserved" barotrauma!), or due to localised air trapping within the lung tissue due to abnormal lung architecture.
- In either case, healing will be by a fibrotic scar in the lung tissue which may predispose to further pulmonary barotrauma.
- Recurrences of pulmonary barotrauma tend to be worse than the first episode.
- *It is strongly recommended not to dive.*

A 25 year old female presented four days after completing a week's diving course. She had performed four dives a day for four days. The dive profiles were within her computer's allowances. She felt very tired, "muddled" in her thinking and had paraesthesia in her legs and face. Decompression illness was diagnosed and she was commenced 100% oxygen and transferred to the local recompression facility where she was given 12 treatments with little improvement. She was classified as a neurological decompression illness with residual sequelae and advised never to dive again.

A 19 year old male performed two deep dives in one day and presented with a niggling shoulder pain and feeling tired. He had no travel insurance and was unwilling to be evacuated and recompressed. He was therefore admitted to the local hospital and given intravenous fluids and 100% oxygen for 6 hours. His symptoms completely subsided and did not recur when the oxygen was stopped. He was classified as a probable musculo-skeletal decompression illness and advised not to dive for four weeks and be more conservative with his diving profiles.

A 31 year old female collapsed 30 minutes after a diving lesson in a 3m (10ft) deep pool. She complained of headache, paraesthesia of both legs and right arm and was noted to be intermittently confused. She was given intravenous fluid, 100% oxygen and improved quickly. She was evacuated for recompression.

Subsequent neurological examination and investigation found no other cause for her symptoms and she was classified as an arterial gas embolism and advised never to dive again.

INNER EAR BAROTRAUMA

points to consider very seriously

- Inner ear barotrauma may involve:
  - haemorrhage into the cochlear duct
  - intralabyrinthine membrane rupture or
  - rupture of the round or oval window membrane which sometimes persists as a fistula.
- Symptoms include vertigo, tinnitus and deafness.
- There are probably many divers who suffer mild and transient symptoms who never seek medical care.
- Once a diver has suffered from inner ear barotrauma they seem more predisposed to repeat episodes.
- Tinnitus and high frequency hearing loss are common long term complications.
- *After any history suggestive of inner ear barotrauma, diving is not recommended until all symptoms have settled, normal hearing has been confirmed and normal Eustachian tube function is demonstrated.*
- *The diver should be advised to equalise their ears very frequently, but not forcibly, whilst diving.*
- *Any diver with persistent symptoms should see an ENT specialist for full assessment.*
- *Following a repair of a round or oval window fistula, it is strongly recommended not to dive.*

Appendix A

CLEARING THE EARS

points to ponder

- A most important function in underwater diving.
- Rupture of the tympanic membrane may occur after a descent of only 1.5 m (5 ft) from the surface.
- Air must travel from the nasopharynx to the middle ear cavity to equalise pressures across the tympanic membrane.
- Techniques to open the Eustachian tube involve pinching the nose, swallowing, blowing into the blocked nose, wiggling the jaw.
- The sensations felt by the diver with opening of the Eustachian tube with pressure equalisation are usually described as a hiss, click, bang, pop or just a feeling of pressure.
- A normal person opens their Eustachian tube on average every second swallow. One swallows about once a minute whilst awake and every five minutes whilst asleep. This does not occur whilst mouth-breathing (eg. through a regulator).
- The major difficulty in "clearing the ears" is due to faulty technique, going too deep too quickly (one should first "clear" the ears within the first 1.5m (5ft)), and not clearing the ears often enough.
- The novice diver should practice "clearing their ears" out of the water 10-20 times per day until they are confident.
- With experience, clearing the ears becomes easier due to better technique and more coordinated musculature around the nasopharynx.
- During a dive, ear clearing may become more difficult due to:
  a) congestion of the nasal mucosa from breathing cold air causing reflex vasodilation of the sub-mucosal venous sinuses;
  b) venous congestion of the sub-mucosal veins from head-down positions encountered during diving;
  c) mucous plugs caused by breathing dry air and reduced swallowing causing nasal mucus to become more viscous; and
  d) mouth-breathing.
- Many divers are initially unable to recognise their ears clearing.

The regular techniques for clearing the ears (in the author's preferred sequence) include:

Toynbee Technique

- Simply pinch the nose and swallow.
- Written up by Joseph Toynbee in 1873.

Valsalva Manoeuvre

- Simply pinch the nostrils, close the mouth and exhale into the nose GENTLY to raise the pressure in the nasopharynx.
- First published in 1704.
- If exhaling is severe or prolonged, the round window can be damaged or even ruptured.
- If exhaling is too severe, the Eustachian tube can be "locked" in a closed position and either refuse to open or open explosively.
- The least pressure is required if the diver is in the vertical position rather than horizontal or head-down.
- If one ear is slow to equalise, it may help to flex the neck laterally to the opposite side.

Modified Valsalva Manoeuvre

- Pinch the nostrils, close the mouth, exhale GENTLY to raise the pressure in the nasopharynx and then swallow.

Remodified Valsalva Manoeuvre

- Pinch the nose, wiggle the jaw from side to side and/or backwards and forwards and swallow. (It looks silly but often works).

Frenzel Manoeuvre

- Close the mouth, nose and glottis (as if about to lift a heavy weight). Force the base of the tongue and the palate against the posterior wall of the nasopharynx (as if starting to say the letter 'K').
- This is a manoeuvre to inflate the Eustachian tube without having to use the pressure effect of the lungs and is independent of breathing.
- Described by Herman Frenzel in 1938.
- Developed for the German Airforce so that their dive bomber pilots could clear their ears.
- There is no danger of round window rupture.

Voluntary Tube Opening

- A controlled contraction of the soft palate and of the upper throat muscles to overcome the normal elasticity of the Eustachian tube, holding the Eustachian tube open for equalisation of pressure.
- First described by French divers and was commonly known as "beance tubaire voluntaire" or BTV.
- The technique is commonly used by experienced divers who seem to gain the technique automatically.

Appendix B

EAR CARE FOR DIVERS

- If ears have a natural tendency to occlude with wax, have them checked regularly, particularly before a prolonged diving trip.
- Do not poke anything into the ears (eg. finger or cotton bud).
- After every dive:
  - Rinse both ears out with fresh water to wash out contaminated water and salt, which is hydrophilic.
  - Instil 2 drops of 5% Acetic Acid in 60% Ethyl Alcohol (or one of the commercial equivalents) into both ears.
  - If very prone to ear infections, blow warm air into the external canal using a hairdryer.

Appendix C

INTERPRETATION OF LUNG FUNCTION TESTS

points to ponder

- Simple respiratory testing has always been accepted as an essential part of the diving medical to try to identify asymptomatic yet significant lung disease.
- The FEV1/FVC ratio has the smallest range of normal variation.
- If a statistical limit of normality of two standard deviations from the mean is applied to the FEV1/FVC ratio, the lower limit of normality would approximate 90% of the predicted values. (As the divers being examined in the 1950's were mainly naval divers between the ages of 18 and 35, the value of 75% became the accepted value of the lower limit of normal).
- If a diver, especially if tall, has large lungs then there may be an abnormally low FEV1/FVC ratio due to dysanapsis of the airways. Because the main expiratory resistance in the normal lung is in the large upper airways, especially the trachea, a diver with large lungs but a slightly small trachea, is unable to exhale as fast as predicted, no matter the state of the smaller airways or the expiratory force applied. However such a diver is in no danger of pulmonary barotrauma through small airway closure.
- Two standard deviations from the mean of FVC and FEV1 measurements would approximate 80% of the predicted values.

- *Any diver with a FVC or FEV1 of less than 60% of predicted should not dive.*
- *Any diver with a FEV1/FVC ratio, FEV1 or a FVC of less than 80% of predicted should be shown to have a normal chest X-ray and bronchial challenge test before diving is permitted.*
- *Any diver with reduced lung function yet no apparent pathology should be advised to ensure that their ascent rate never exceeds 10m/min (33ft/min).*

Appendix D

STANDARD DIVING MEDICAL TEXTBOOKS

Edmonds C, Lowry C and Pennefather J.
Diving and Subaquatic Medicine (3rd edition).
London: Butterworth Heinemann, 1992.
ISBN 0-7506-0259-7

Bove AA and Davis JC.
Diving Medicine (2nd edition).
Philadelphia: Saunders, 1990.
ISBN 0-7216-2934-2

Schilling CW, Carlson CB and Mathias RA (eds).
The Physician's Guide to Diving Medicine.
New York: Plenum Press, 1984.
ISBN 0-306-41428-7

Bennett PB and Elliott DH (eds).
The Physiology and Medicine of Diving (4th edition).
London: W.B. Saunders Co Ltd, 1993.
ISBN 0-7020-1589-X

Appendix E

UNDERWATER MEDICAL SOCIETIES

Membership to the diving medical societies is recommended to keep up to date and broaden your knowledge.

Undersea and Hyperbaric Medical Society (UHMS)
9650 Rockville Pike,
Bethesda,
Maryland 20814.
U.S.A.

A society for hyperbaric and diving medical doctors and associates with an emphasis on pure research, commercial diving and hyperbaric medicine.
It is the most prestigious of all the diving medical societies.

It publishes a chatty and informative newsletter "Pressure" (ISSN 0889-0242) and a quarterly journal entitled "Undersea and Hyperbaric Medicine"
 (ISSN 0093-5387).

European Underwater and Baromedical Society (EUBS)
c/o Mrs A. Randell,
6 Parkhill Avenue,
Dyce, Aberdeen,
AB2 OFP, Scotland.

The European counterpart to the American based UHMS.
It publishes a two-monthly newsletter, "EUBS Newsletter"

South Pacific Underwater Medicine Society (SPUMS)
c/o Australian and New Zealand College of Anaesthetists,
Spring Street,
Melbourne,
Victoria 3000,
Australia.

A society of doctors and associates interested in underwater medicine with a special emphasis on sports medicine, but also covering hyperbaric medicine.
Its very readable quarterly journal, "SPUMS Journal" (ISSN 0813-1988) is full of opinion and fact and helps keep up to date, especially with sports diving medicine.

Appendix F

INTERNATIONAL DIVERS ALERT NETWORK (IDAN)

An organisation originating in the USA but which now has affiliated organisations around the world. It fulfils many roles, which include:

- collecting data on diving practises and accidents for analysis and research.
- supplying routine and emergency information to divers and diving doctors.
- providing an insurance cover for divers.
- assisting in emergency transport and repatriation for injured divers.
- publishing a chatty and informative newsletter "Alert Diver".
- providing training in emergency oxygen first aid for divers.

Membership is recommended.

Further enquiries should be made to:

International Divers Alert Network Headquarters,
Box 3823, Duke University Medical Centre,
Durham, N.C. 27710, USA.

DAN America,
Box 3823, Duke University Medical Centre,
Durham, N.C. 27710, USA.

DAN Australasia,
PO Box 134, Carnegie Vic. 3163, Australia.

DAN Europe,
Via Puglie 82, 64026 Roseto Abruzzi, Italy.

DAN Japan,
Tokyo Medical and Dental University,
I-chome, Yushima, Bunkyo-ku, Tokyo 113 Japan.

Appendix G

DIVING EMERGENCY FACILITIES AROUND THE WORLD

AUSTRALIA:
DES Australia, ph. 1-800-088200 from within Australia (free call)
61-8-373-5312 from elsewhere.
08-222-5116 for non-urgent information.

CANADA:
Toronto General Hospital Hyperbaric Unit, ph. 416-3404131.

EUROPE:
DAN Europe Central Hotline, Rega-Zurich (multilingual), ph. 41-1-383-1111.

DAN Europe Deutschland, ph. 0431-54090
(ask for Diving Doctor on call – German speaking).

DAN Europe Italy, ph. 39-85-8930333.

DAN Europe Malta, ph. 09-94193.

DAN Europe Spain, ph. 93-4331551.

In **France**, dial 15, the Emergency Medical Services National Number.

Note of caution: Unless fluent in any local language, call DAN Europe Central Hotline in Zurich. The DAN Europe protocol will be activated and the appropriate national hotlines and hyperbaric facilities alerted and co-ordinated.

JAPAN:
DAN Japan ph. 81-3-3812-4999.

NEW ZEALAND:
DES New Zealand, ph. 64-9-445-8454

UNITED KINGDOM:
HMAS Nelson/Gunwharf (Vernon), ph. 0705-818888
or Diving Disease Research Centre on Plymouth
ph. 0752-261910 (24-hr emergencies) 0752-408093 (9am-5pm weekdays)

UNITED STATES OF AMERICA:
DAN USA,
ph. 919-6848111 for emergencies, 919-6842948 for non-urgent information.

Acknowledgements

The author gratefully acknowledges advice, support and help from (in alphabetical order):

Dr. Lindsay Barker

Dr. Elizabeth Clark

Dr. Llew Davies

Dr. Bill Douglas

Dr. Carl Edmonds

Dr. Tom Fallowfield

Dr. Des Gorman

Dr. Mikal Kluger

Dr. John Knight

Dr. Chris Lowry (the other one)

Dr. Janene Mannerheim

Dr. Alessandro Marroni

Dr. Richard Moon

Dr. Brennon O'Dempsey

Dr. Harry Oxer

Dr. John Reimer

Dr. Michael Rooney

Dr. David Vissenga

Dr. John Williamson

Dr. Peter Wilmshurst

Dr. Roger Wilson

and the patience and understanding of his wife Rose and his publisher John Lippmann (in that order!).

Biography

Dr. John Parker trained to scuba dive in 1967 whilst studying medicine at Edinburgh University, Scotland. He escaped the hypothermic Scottish waters to explore the Great Barrier Reef in 1975. During his travels he became an advanced diving instructor, managed a dive shop and school in Brisbane, Australia and ran all the diving on Keppel Island on the central Queensland coast for six months. In 1977 he was the diving doctor at the World Underwater Congress diving expedition on Heron Island.

John has studied diving medicine at the Underwater School of Medicine at HMAS Penguin in Sydney, Australia, the Hyperbaric Unit, Royal Adelaide Hospital in South Australia and at the National Hyperbaric Centre in Aberdeen, Scotland.

He has been running a busy diving medical/general practice in the Whitsunday Island area of Queensland since 1979 and has published several papers on the sports diving medical.

John is still an active diver and has logged over 3000 dives.

Index

Other books available from J. L. Publications

The DES/DAN Emergency Handbook
by John Lippmann and Stan Bugg. Melbourne: J. L. Publications, 1990.
A guide to the identification of and first aid for scuba diving injuries.

Deeper Into Diving
by John Lippmann. Melbourne: J. L. Publications, 1990.
A detailed technical review of most of the available decompression procedures and of the physical and physiological aspects of deeper diving.

The Essentials of Deeper Sport Diving
by John Lippmann. New York: Aqua Quest Publications Inc., 1992.
An overview of the theory and requirements of deeper diving.

Oxygen First Aid for Divers
by John Lippmann. Melbourne: J. L. Publications, 1992.
The most comprehensive guide to oxygen administration to injured divers, written in plain language.

Diving Medicine for Scuba Divers
by Drs. Carl Edmonds, Bart McKenzie and Robert Thomas.
Melbourne: J. L. Publications, 1992.
Diving Medicine explained by experts in clear and simple terms, and in a very interesting and entertaining manner.

Scuba Safety in Australia
edited by Dr. Jeff Wilks, Dr. John Knight and John Lippmann.
Melbourne: J. L. Publications, 1993.
A comprehensive review of various aspects of recreational diving safety.

J. L. Publications
PO Box 381, Carnegie, Victoria 3163
Australia
Tel/Fax: 61-3-569 4803
